THE PLAYFUL MIND

HOW TO RESTORE THE HAPPINESS WE EXPERIENCED AS CHILDREN

PAUL DANIEL

CONTENTS

INTRODUCTION
THE PLAYFUL MIND IS A HAPPY MIND

When we were children, it was much easier to engage with the present moment and be happy. As we got older, we still try to do this, but it's become much harder.

What changed between being a child and being an adult? It was the ease with which we entered the "playful mind". The playful mind is a mentality that is *receptive* to *engaging* with the moment. The more open we are to engaging with the present, the easier it is to feel happy and satisfied. This state lets us get the most out of each moment. Without it, we struggle to connect deeply with what we're doing. This disconnect makes it much harder to feel those emotions.

Why did we find it easier to enter the playful mind as children than as adults? As we got older, our ability to generate this mindset was *interfered* with. This book aims to *remove* these sources of interference so that it becomes easier to generate this playful mentality — even as adults. Following this, we'll find it easier to feel consistently happy and satisfied.

So what are the sources of interference? And how do we remove them?

THE *PRIMARY* SOURCES OF INTERFERENCE WITH THE PLAYFUL MIND

The primary sources of interference are the mental frameworks we've adopted while growing up that either (a) inhibit our satisfaction or (b) cause us to suffer. These are two broad types of thought patterns that can adversely affect our emotional state. While they may sound similar, these mental frameworks operate a little differently from one another.

A *mental framework inhibits our satisfaction* when it lowers the enjoyment we'd otherwise get from an activity. We can have thoughts during a pastime — like listening to a band we like — that corrode the joy we feel while doing it. Sometimes our satisfaction is completely blocked; other times, we feel some enjoyment, but it's far less than what it could be. Without these thoughts, such pastimes would be much more fun and engaging.

A *mental framework causes us to suffer* when it leads to emotional pain and distress. These ways of thinking can trigger low self-esteem or despair when we don't get what we want. Much of this thinking is ego-driven, making us feel powerless and angry about past events. Without these thoughts, we wouldn't suffer as much, even when undesirable things happen. Our memories don't have to be a source of pain.

Both mental frameworks disrupt the formation of the playful mind. We become less open to engaging with the present when our own thoughts block our satisfaction or cause emotional pain. When we suffer, our attention shifts to that suffering instead of the activity in front of us.

Anyone who has adopted these mental frameworks should try to remove them if they want to be happier. To appreciate the value of doing this, imagine two people: one with these thought patterns and one without. Both can be listening to music they like, but only one has their enjoyment blocked. Both can go through the same unpleasant event, but only one suffers deeply. *The other may not suffer at all.* In both cases, it's their way of thinking that changes how much satisfaction or suffering they experience.

So how do we remove these mental frameworks from the mind?

We have to dismantle them. To "dismantle" a framework is to identify contradictions in its core logic. We're unlikely to keep applying a pattern of thinking once we no longer see it as logically consistent. Such a pattern can only really sustain itself in our minds if we believe its core logic is internally sound. By exposing its flaws, we break that logic, which makes it unable to hold itself together.

Frameworks that we have discarded for being contradictory will not disrupt the playful mind or our engagement with the present. The more of these thought patterns we undo, the more we can enjoy each moment, and the less susceptible we become to suffering. How we break these forms of thinking and more will be covered in:

- Chapter 1 – Dismantling Mental Frameworks That Inhibit Our Satisfaction
- Chapter 2 – Dismantling Mental Frameworks That Cause Us Suffering
- Chapter 3 — Stopping Ourselves from Recalling Unwanted Memories

To be clear, there may be events where suffering feels like the only possible response. But it's always worth asking whether the anguish is actually coming from a thought pattern we're following that contains deep contradictions. Sure, reacting with emotional suffering to a particular event may be understandable and well within the ordinary range of human reactions. But is there a chance that it is completely unnecessary? Is it possible that this suffering is not an inevitable response?

We may believe it is inevitable, especially when so many people around us react to events with anguish. But most people have only been taught how to adopt mental frameworks that lead to suffering, rather than how to dismantle them. They've been given blueprints for how to think, but never taught how to question the design or rebuild it. They have not been shown how to properly reshape and navigate their own minds.

Broadly speaking, getting into the habit of breaking these frameworks trains us to avoid suffering. However, that is an overly simplistic characterization. More precisely, it helps us *avoid creating our own suffering* in that we stop applying harmful mental patterns.

THE *SECONDARY* SOURCE OF INTERFERENCE WITH THE PLAYFUL MIND

The secondary source of interference is our drive to arrive at a complete model of reality.

Our "model of reality" is our understanding of what reality is and how it works, based on our observations so far. Our aim is to make this model as *consistent* with those observations as possible. However, our preoccupation with building this understanding can make it harder to deeply engage with the present. We become so concerned with answering questions about existence that we struggle to enter the playful mind and connect with what's right in front of us.

As children, our brains weren't fully developed, so the questions we had about reality were relatively simple. We were satisfied with the simple answers we received, and even if we had heard more complex ones, we wouldn't have understood them. But as we grew older and our brains became more sophisticated, our minds organically began to formulate more complex questions about reality. This was accompanied by an intensifying desire to find answers. We also found it harder to fulfill this desire, as the answers we were given became increasingly difficult to accept or feel satisfied with.

How do we stop this drive from disrupting the playful mind as an adult?

We cannot remove this interference simply by "dismantling" our model of reality. Identifying its contradictions doesn't eliminate the deeper urge to form a coherent understanding of how things work. It's this strong impulse that preoccupies us and makes it harder to engage with the present. Nor do I believe we should eliminate that urge entirely. We still need a coherent conception of reality that aligns with our observed experiences. After all, reaching our goals depends on recognizing the causal relationships in reality that we can act on.

The best way to prevent this drive from disrupting our engagement with the present is to complete *enough* of the model. A "complete enough" version is not exhaustive in explaining how reality works, but it provides enough answers to satisfy us. Once we consider this drive sufficiently fulfilled, we tend to relax and no longer feel the same urgency to keep expanding the model. We will still continue learning about reality, but more of our attention will shift toward engaging with the present as it arises. From this place of relaxation, it is much easier to approach each moment with the playful mind.

What counts as a "complete enough" model of reality can vary from person to person. People relax at different levels of completeness. Some are satisfied with relatively little, while others need much more. In this book, we'll explore what I consider a sufficiently complete and satisfying version for most people. In my view, reaching that point requires us to grasp the "foundational building blocks" in enough detail. These core components are what everything else we observe in reality is situated upon. Like the foundations of a house, they support everything else that is built on top of them. It is a lot easier for us to relax about questions of existence when we bring what is foundational to sufficient resolution.

The core building blocks we'll cover in this book include our sense of right and wrong, the definition of life, and how to best cultivate satisfaction in our relationships, whether they are romantic, familial, or friendly. Such details will be covered in:

- Chapter 4 – How We Build Our Model of Reality
- Chapter 5 – The Foundational Beliefs in Our Model of Reality
- Chapter 6 – How We Understand What Is Right and Wrong

AFTER REMOVING THIS INTERFERENCE, IS MORE ACTION NEEDED TO GENERATE THE PLAYFUL MIND?

No, we don't need to do anything extra. Just like when we were children, the *default* mental state to be in is that of the playful mind. With the interference gone, we *automatically* become mentally open to engaging with the present. As a result, we become much more efficient at generating happiness and other satisfying feelings from each moment. It takes much less conscious effort to produce these feelings. By removing unhelpful patterns of thought, we also clear out unnecessary mental chatter. This makes our interaction with the present much cleaner and more direct.

I see removing this interference with our playful mind as us resetting our mental state to its "original factory settings". At this point, we can easily bring the playful mind to almost everything we do, even things we would usually consider "mundane". The playful mind is always trying to emerge because it's the optimal mental state for drawing happiness and contentment from our experiences. We just need to stop getting in its way.

To be clear, we're not resetting everything to factory settings; instead, we are reclaiming our ability to be playful and engage with the present moment. For example, we're not trying to revert to a child's level of moral reasoning or sense of responsibility. That would not be good for our happiness.

WHAT COMES NEXT THEN?

As mentioned, the playful mind helps us extract happiness and other gratifying emotions from what we're doing. When the mind is free from interference and can engage with almost anything, happiness is produced more reliably from one instance to the next. But what determines the *mix of other satisfying feelings* that accompany it?

It depends on the specific activity we're engaged in. For example, when we are floating in a calm ocean, we may feel tranquility and peace. Or when dancing at a concert, we may feel fun and excitement. Without the playful mind, we can still experience these kinds of emotions, though only in smaller amounts. With the playful mind, not only do we feel them more deeply, but we also experience happiness alongside them. This blend of feelings *complements* and *enhances* the happiness we're already experiencing.

In my view, our goal is not just to attain happiness. It's also about exploring how our happiness can be enhanced by other satisfying feelings that come from deep engagement with the moment. This means extending the playful mind to as many activities as possible to see what different combinations of enjoyable emotions arise.

Over time, through experience and experimentation, we'll start to identify which pursuits trigger specific satisfying feelings. This insight becomes useful when we're in the mood to enhance our happiness with a particular emotion. We select what to do in order to actively shape our overall happiness, effectively curating how we feel at that moment in time. The process of identifying the right pursuits will be explored in "Chapter 11 – Triggering Specific Feelings to Enhance Our Happiness".

To be clear, there are times when we are not too picky about which satisfying feelings we want to enhance our happiness with. We're content with whatever arises and aren't seeking anything specific. As a result, we don't actively try to shape our overall happiness by targeting particular activities. We can just let things be.

A COMMON MISCONCEPTION ABOUT HOW TO ATTAIN HAPPINESS

A common theory is that pursuing and attaining external things — such as success, fame, money, and romantic love — will lead to happiness. Many people who don't consider themselves happy believe it's simply because they haven't yet acquired all the external things they desire.

If happiness did indeed work this way, there wouldn't be so many successful actors and musicians who see themselves as being unhappy. Such people, who would widely be considered to "have it all" in terms of external achievements, can still be depressed and even suicidal. Their experiences should serve as a warning to the rest of us: simply having these external things does not automatically make one happy. After all, these people are actually *testing the theory* that external pursuits are the primary drivers of happiness.

In my view, the reason these people are unhappy is simple. While they were busy chasing external things, they did not work on improving what actually drives happiness most — their mental state. They did not spend enough time undoing the thought patterns that block their contentment and cause anguish. They did not build a model of reality that was coherent enough to bring them peace of mind. It does not matter how many external things we attain — how rich and successful we become — if we do not have a mentality that allows us to enjoy them. When we shift our mental state, we will find that we can be very happy without many of these external things.

More and more people — famous or not — are turning to psychology and philosophy to solve the problem of unhappiness. This trend suggests a growing recognition that our mindset plays a key role in both satisfaction and suffering. From my perspective, psychology and philosophy are fundamentally about the same thing: examining our mental frameworks to reduce suffering and create happiness. Both focus on changing our mentality. They just go about it in different ways and are couched in different terminology.

What I am offering in this book is the approach that worked for me. This is an approach I only came to understand because I was suffering myself. The pain became so unbearable that I had little choice but to find what the cause was. At first, I believed my unhappiness came from unwanted events in my life or from not having attained specific external goals. But as I looked deeper, it became clear that my suffering was caused by my mental state. I had taken on thought patterns that were diminishing my enjoyment and causing me emotional pain. I also hadn't resolved enough key existential questions, which made it hard to relax and stay open to the present.

So, when you read this book, I don't want you to think I'm speaking about these matters from a distance. I understand all of this only because it was once how I thought and felt. I'm not sitting above in judgment. Fortunately, I became so familiar with these harmful thought patterns that I learned how to break their core logic. In doing so, I believe I took the most direct path to resolving the problem of unhappiness because I addressed its root cause.

Everyone should pursue whatever approach works best for them. However, many approaches I've seen tend to focus on suppressing destructive thought patterns or addressing only surface-level issues. Because they don't deal with the root cause directly, these approaches often become overly philosophical, circling around the heart of the issue without confronting it. Some methods may seem simpler, but they still don't eliminate the problem; they merely hide it. If we want a more streamlined way of thinking that generates happiness more effectively, we have to examine and dismantle the cumbersome mental machinery we've built over the years. We must confront the harmful thinking that limits us — not ignore it or skirt around the edges — if we want to experience genuine mental freedom and deeper happiness.

THE SECTIONS OF THIS BOOK

This book can be separated into two sections.

The first section is about removing interference with the playful mind so it can be generated with less conscious effort. This section comprises Chapters 1-10.

The second section is about understanding how to use specific feelings to enhance the happiness we produce from the playful mind. This section comprises Chapter 11 only.

1

—————

DISMANTLING MENTAL FRAMEWORKS THAT INHIBIT OUR SATISFACTION

Mental frameworks that inhibit our satisfaction often come from the *ego*. This part of us can block our enjoyment when it thinks we'll look *foolish* to others for genuinely liking or valuing a particular activity. This thought pattern can adversely affect everyday experiences like listening to a specific genre of music or watching a TV show or film.

Our ego can be so worried about how we appear that it shuts us off from fully enjoying the experience. Even if we're innately drawn to something, the ego might hold us back. It can stop us from entering the playful mind. Without that open mindset, it's harder to feel happiness and other satisfying emotions while doing the activity. We might even avoid trying it at all. When the ego thinks this way, we can be said to have adopted a framework that limits our enjoyment. So how do we dismantle this thought pattern and keep it from getting in the way?

We can't dismantle the ego to the point that it no longer exists; it will always be part of us. But we can understand its concern about looking foolish and break the logic behind it. Once that logic is broken, the concern loses its grip. With this thought pattern gone, the ego no longer interferes with our ability to enjoy or value what we're doing.

The core logic of this worry is that we shouldn't do anything that seems foolish, regardless of whether it truly is or just appears that way. But who is the *greater fool*: someone who genuinely enjoys something others might find silly, or someone who cares so much about appearances that they block their own happiness? If we let this worry get in our way, we're allowing it to interfere with what matters most to us. Sacrificing our happiness just to protect our image is one of the most misguided choices we can make. In trying not to look foolish to others, we give up something that makes us the greater fool in the end.

When the ego recognizes the contradiction in worrying about appearing foolish, it stops caring as much about what others think. This makes it easier for us to genuinely enjoy and value what we do, unaffected by whether others see it as silly. Deep down, we all want to enjoy and value what we're innately drawn to without being held back by others' opinions. So it shouldn't be too difficult for the ego to let go of this concern.

I want to point out here that our blocked enjoyment isn't really caused by other people. They aren't the ones "controlling" what we can and can't enjoy; *our own ego is doing that*. More precisely, it's the ego's worry about appearing foolish that gets in the way. When we dismantle the logic behind that worry, we remove a major barrier to our satisfaction.

Since the ego is what limits our gratification, the real question isn't how to stop others from "controlling" what we enjoy, but rather how to stop our own ego from doing so. Its concerns don't come from a well-reasoned or practical place. They stem from insecurity and paranoia about how we're perceived. Should we really let our satisfaction be controlled by something so unstable and fearful?

Just to be clear: I'm not suggesting we make ourselves completely oblivious to whether people think we are foolish or not. There are plenty of instances where we would not want specific individuals to see us this way, as they can become obstacles to something we're pursuing. For example, when going for a job promotion, how decision-makers view us can directly impact our chances. It can make sense in these situations to be extra careful about what we disclose about ourselves.

What I'm really suggesting is that we don't let worries about how we're perceived affect our sincere enjoyment of what we do in our personal time. Even if we decide not to share what we do in private, our ego's worry that it seems foolish can still limit our enjoyment. For example, even if I don't tell anyone that I like a particular band, my ego — convinced others would judge me for it — can still diminish the experience. But our enjoyment being blocked can only happen *if we let it*. Personally, I don't mind sharing things about myself that I suspect others might see as silly. And I believe most people, deep down, want to be open and express themselves freely, without worrying about what others think.

So far, we've explored arguments for breaking down a *general* mental framework that can limit our satisfaction. We'll now look at how to undo this thought pattern for *types of activities* where the ego feels especially uneasy about how we're perceived.

TYPE #1: THE ACTIVITY HAS FLAWED MOMENTS

In this case, the ego is nervous about appearing foolish for enjoying or valuing something with noticeable flaws. When we engage with any form of media — like a film — we typically apply a "critical lens" to each moment. Through this lens, we identify elements that "don't work" for us and regard them as flaws. In a film, these might include the dialogue, plot, acting, music, and so on.

We also have an "appreciative lens" that we can apply. This lens helps us recognize the elements that "do work". We're able to generate satisfying feelings during a pastime by engaging with the parts that are well-executed. In a film, for example, we can experience a lot of enjoyment from scenes where the dialogue, plot, acting, and music come together effectively.

Sometimes, *all* the elements in a given moment work well for us, and we feel deeply satisfied. Other times, some are well-executed while others are not. For example, the dialogue and acting might be effective, but the plot and music may be lacking. Even when some parts fall short, we can still stay open to enjoying what does work.

A problem arises when our ego becomes worried about appearing foolish for enjoying something that has flaws. When we notice elements in a moment that don't work, the ego's fear of looking silly can keep us from engaging with the parts that do. We may become mentally blocked from appreciating the *rest of the elements in that same moment*. This happens even when those components are well-executed and could bring us enjoyment if we simply allowed ourselves to engage. For example, we might be watching a film and come across a scene where the dialogue falls flat. Since our ego is nervous about appearing foolish for enjoying it, we become so mentally closed off to the film that we overlook the other elements — plot, acting, and music — that are working well in that same scene. In this instance, our enjoyment has been blocked.

When the ego's worry is high, even a minor flaw can make us completely unreceptive to the well-executed elements in that moment. This nervousness can grow so strong that we mentally shut off not only to the present elements but also to those in *later parts of the activity*. As a result, our satisfaction in future moments is also diminished. For example, we might react to a small flaw in the dialogue of one scene by becoming unreceptive to the dialogue, plot, acting, and music in later scenes, even when those aspects are working well. We might become so mentally closed off that we can't even recognize the elements that are performing well. We only see what doesn't.

When our ego is only mildly concerned about seeming foolish, a flaw has to be more significant before we mentally shut down to the elements that are well-executed. When this insecurity is small, we won't let a minor flaw — like a weak line of dialogue — stop us from enjoying the plot, acting, or music that still resonate, whether in that scene or later on. When our ego isn't too worried, we can recognize faults while still maintaining enough mental openness to engage with what works. This ability to stay receptive, even while noticing imperfections, helps us feel more satisfied throughout the experience.

What I find interesting is that when we don't enjoy something, we often assume it's because of the flaws we've noticed. We blame the activity itself, when in reality, it's often our ego's worry about appearing foolish for genuinely enjoying it. That concern causes us to mentally shut off from the parts that do work. In this way, the ego blocks our gratification.

To free our ego from this concern, we must recognize that clinging to this worry is choosing to be the greater fool. When we hold on to this worry, we let it limit the happiness and satisfaction we could experience throughout the activity. The less foolish thing to do would be to drop this concern, allowing more moments in which we can feel happy and satisfied. At the very least, we shouldn't be working to reduce the enjoyable parts of our lives.

TYPE #2: THE ACTIVITY IS NOT "IMPORTANT"

In this case, the ego worries about looking foolish for enjoying or valuing an activity when it is not considered "important". Our mental openness to engage with something can be heavily affected by whether we consider it important. If we cannot frame it as being vital in some way, we may find it difficult to engage with, and our enjoyment can be significantly restricted while doing the activity.

To be clear, even if the ego didn't exist, we would still struggle to stay mentally open to engaging with something we view as unimportant. But if, on top of that, the ego also worries about looking silly for enjoying it, this *further* blocks our ability to engage, which *further* limits the enjoyment we might otherwise feel.

Many of us define "importance" in terms of scale of impact. A pursuit that affects a large number of people is often seen as important. When we recognize that something has broad impact, we're more likely to be mentally receptive to engaging with it, thereby increasing our ability to draw satisfaction from it.

A problem arises when we define importance solely in terms of large-scale impact and don't recognize other ways something can matter to us. As a result, we may struggle to stay mentally open to engaging with pursuits that don't affect many people, simply because we don't see them as important. This makes it harder to enjoy them. Yet most of our daily life is spent doing things that don't have a broad impact. When we rely on such a narrow definition of importance, it becomes difficult to feel satisfied during much of our everyday experience.

Another challenge arises when we assume that the only scale of impact that matters is a *global* one. As a result, even projects that significantly affect a local community, state, or country — each arguably large-scale in its own right — may be dismissed as unimportant simply because they don't impact the entire world. This perspective may not only diminish our sense of fulfillment in doing such things but also discourage us from pursuing them at all, despite the clear benefits they offer to many.

We can get around this problem by recognizing what I think is a more fundamental definition of what is important to us. In my view, what makes something fundamentally matter to us is that it *affects our satisfaction*. As such, *every moment* we have matters because every moment affects our satisfaction. And *every activity* we do matters because they all affect the satisfaction in these moments. Such is the case, even if what we're doing isn't having a large-scale or global impact. This includes things like chatting to a friend, going to the beach, or just sitting on our own and having a quiet moment. With this mindset, we recognize the *fundamental importance* of each moment and activity. This substantially increases our mental receptivity to engage with everything we do, which in turn boosts the enjoyment we feel throughout each day.

By challenging the idea that only large-scale impact defines importance, we stop framing everything we do in terms of its potential for large-scale results. This allows us to explore and discover the intricate details of each moment as they emerge, free from such considerations of scale. We can enjoy the moment for its own sake, as opposed to thinking about some other goal that it could be or should be serving instead. Each point in time can be experienced without constantly assessing it against some external measure of scale.

For example, when we go to the beach, we can enjoy the feeling of sand between our toes and the smell of the sea without worrying about how we're only benefiting ourselves at that point in time. We can chat with a friend and enjoy the conversation without feeling we should be doing something more far-reaching. In my view, any contempt we have for what we call "mundane" comes from us narrowly defining importance in terms of scale of impact. Once we stop thinking so much in these terms, it becomes easier to appreciate the quiet moments. To me, these are some of the most satisfying experiences we have. They are also among the most common.

Just to be clear: we're not limited to a single way of recognizing importance. Different things can be important for different reasons. I'm not trying to dissuade anyone from pursuing things that have large-scale impacts, but they're not the only things that matter. In any case, I think the reason we often see large-scale endeavors as important is that they affect not just people, but more specifically, their levels of satisfaction. The endeavor matters because it shapes the satisfaction and suffering of many.

Strictly speaking, none of the above reasoning is about convincing ourselves or our ego to be mentally open to engaging with things we consider unimportant. It's more about challenging the basis on which we label such pursuits as "unimportant" in the first place. Yes, we may see some things as more important than others, but each holds fundamental value because, as discussed, it affects our satisfaction. Recognizing this helps us remain mentally open to engaging with whatever we're doing.

TYPE #3: THE ACTIVITY IS NOT THE BEST ONE

In this case, the ego is uneasy about appearing foolish for *missing out* on the best pursuit. When we're doing something we don't see as the best option, our thoughts can become so preoccupied with what else we could be doing that we become unreceptive to the present moment. In other words, the fear of missing out pulls our attention away from the current experience, and as a result, we feel less satisfaction from it.

Our ego can be so uneasy about missing out on the best option that even shifting to something clearly better doesn't resolve it. It has to be the best. Otherwise, we're likely to remain distracted by thoughts of an even more rewarding possibility we might be missing. We'd still be mentally closed off to this better pursuit, and our enjoyment would remain blocked.

It would seem that one way to address this concern about missing out is to find the best option. So how do we do that? First, we need to articulate what it actually means for something to be the "best". I think for many people, it boils down to what delivers the *greatest* satisfaction. Things that are highly satisfying yet fall short of that benchmark can't truly be considered the best. While this criteria seems straightforward, finding such an activity is complicated for a number of reasons.

One challenge is that comparing two activities in terms of overall satisfaction isn't always easy, primarily because it's often unclear which one truly offers more. Each experience can produce a unique blend of satisfying emotions as it unfolds. One might bring more peace, tranquility, and calm, while another offers more excitement, adventure, and delight. At times, it's possible to tell that one brings more overall satisfaction than another. But in my experience, most pursuits tend to offer similar levels of gratification — just in different forms. When I compare them, the types of enjoyment they provide feel more like apples and oranges.

Another factor is that the mix of satisfying feelings we experience isn't determined solely by the activity itself. While the nature of the undertaking does shape the range of enjoyable emotions available to us, we can't fully access that range unless we're in the playful mind. If we keep assuming the experience depends only on the activity — and overlook the role of our mentality — we won't take steps to shift the mindset. As a result, we'll keep bringing a closed-off mentality to everything we do and continue missing out on happiness and a fuller range of satisfying emotions.

By approaching nearly everything we take part in — even the so-called "mundane" — with the playful mind, we can elevate those experiences to a much higher level of satisfaction. The more often we do this, the harder it becomes to compare experiences in terms of which offers "more" or "less" gratification. Each activity can provide a high level of satisfaction, just in different ways. When describing two such experiences, we're more likely to say they're "different" rather than "better" or "worse".

As we begin to experience high levels of gratification across a wide range of endeavors through the playful mind, it becomes clear that no single pursuit consistently offers the most. There is no one "best" thing, only a variety of experiences that provide deep fulfillment in different ways. Searching for the one ideal pursuit doesn't make much sense, because it likely doesn't exist.

Even if something truly is the best because it offers the greatest satisfaction, we might not recognize it when we find it. And even if we do, we can't confirm that something better doesn't exist elsewhere, which can leave us feeling like we're still missing out. We might remain distracted by thoughts of a better experience that exists only as pure fantasy. This distraction can close us off to what is genuinely most fulfilling. So even in the "best-case scenario", where we've found something deeply satisfying, our ego's fear of missing out can still block our enjoyment.

I don't think it matters much if the absolute best activity exists and we never do it, because we can still find high levels of gratification in many things. But when the ego fears missing out, we close ourselves off to the present moment and limit our ability to draw deep contentment from it. We can become so distracted by the idea of a *hypothetical* best pursuit that we fail to engage with the details of the one we're actually in. Ironically, our concern about missing out on what life has to offer can cause us to keep missing what's happening right in front of us. Only the greater fool would let the search for the "best" make them overlook the rich satisfaction available in everything else.

When we let go of this ego-driven fixation, the distraction fades, and we start to notice the details unfolding in the present. It also becomes easier to see each activity on its own terms, rather than constantly comparing it to some hypothetical best. As a result, everything we do becomes much more enjoyable.

WATCH FOR OTHER ACTIVITIES THE EGO FIXATES ON

What's been discussed in this chapter doesn't cover every type of pursuit the ego might worry about. I have focused specifically on the most common ones that, in my view, most strongly reduce our enjoyment.

I suspect each of us has other pursuits our ego fixates on, though we may not always be aware of them. To help the ego let go of these worries and stop them from blocking our gratification, we first need to identify what they are. That's not always easy. A good place to start is by asking ourselves: *What would I genuinely enjoy if I weren't afraid of looking foolish?* We can also try to imagine how we'd approach these things as children, free from ego-driven concerns and with fewer inhibitions.

2

—————

DISMANTLING MENTAL FRAMEWORKS THAT CAUSE US SUFFERING

When something undesirable happens to us, the emotional suffering we experience depends on the mental frameworks we apply. The same event can happen to two people, yet their levels of distress can vary greatly depending on the thought patterns they've adopted. One person may suffer deeply, while the other may not suffer at all. The more we adopt frameworks that generate suffering, the more mentally vulnerable we become to emotional pain.

The emotional distress caused by these mental frameworks can interfere with having a playful mind. Without this playful mentality, it becomes harder to experience happiness and other satisfying emotions that come from engaging with the present. By dismantling these frameworks — by spotting contradictions in their logic — we become less prone to suffering. With less suffering, there's less interference with the playful mind. As we become less vulnerable to emotional pain, we can relax, and the playful mindset comes more easily from that relaxed state.

To be clear: just because we've learned how to break these mental frameworks doesn't mean it's impossible for us to adopt them again. It's just much harder to do so, since part of our mind now recognizes the flaw in their logic. A disrupted framework has a harder time holding itself together. And even if we slip back into it and feel the pain again, it will be easier to discard, as we just have to remind ourselves of the contradiction. Each time we dismantle these mental frameworks, we train the mind to get better at breaking their logic and at avoiding self-created emotional pain.

In Chapter 1, we explored how to undo mental frameworks that block our enjoyment, specifically those shaped by ego-driven thinking. In Chapter 2, we'll be dismantling mental frameworks that cause emotional anguish, primarily those related to *self-worth* and *ego*.

Most of us understand, at least on some level, that emotional suffering is often tied to these parts of ourselves. This is why, when we suffer, we commonly refer to ourselves as having "self-worth issues" and "ego issues". In this chapter, we'll first look at breaking down thought patterns related to the former, then move on to those tied to the latter.

HOW TO GET OUR SELF-WORTH BACK

There are two types of self-worth we can feel.

There is what I would call "tethered self-worth". When we've been conditioned to tether our self-esteem to a *specific outcome*, we feel a sense of personal worth when that objective is reached. For example, we might link our self-worth to winning running events, so that coming first triggers a temporary surge of value.

We also have what I'd call "instinctive self-worth". This is the kind of self-esteem we *intrinsically* felt as children. We felt it automatically, without needing to reflect on whether we met any standard of value. We didn't have to do anything in particular to feel confident in ourselves — it existed independently of our actions.

How Our Feelings of Self-Esteem Evolved as We Got Older

At the start of childhood, *all we had was instinctive self-worth*. We generated it easily and without effort. At that stage, we didn't tie our self-esteem to any specific outcome. Our brains likely weren't developed enough to be conditioned that way. For example, we couldn't yet link our personal value to coming first in a race.

As our brains developed — still during early childhood — we began learning from those around us to attach our self-worth to specific goals. Not just one goal, but many, across both physical and mental activities. We began adopting mental measures of personal value. From then on, when we completed a task and got the desired result, we started to feel tethered self-worth.

It may seem, on the surface, like a good thing that we were conditioned to tie our self-esteem to objectives, since it appears to increase the satisfaction we get from our efforts. But the problem with being conditioned this way from a young age is that it leads us to subconsciously believe we're only *deserving of worth* when we reach specific outcomes. And when we don't — like failing to come first in a race — we feel undeserving. Put simply, we start to believe, deep down, that we're *fundamentally worthless.*

When we start to believe we're fundamentally worthless, we also start to *feel* that way. As long as we carry this view of ourselves, we carry the unpleasant emotions that come with it. Even when we reach the goals we've tied our self-worth to, it doesn't erase the underlying belief in our worthlessness. Despite seeing ourselves as deserving when we meet those objectives, we still believe, deep down, that our default state is to be without worth. Reaching those goals hasn't changed what we believe about our intrinsic value.

That said, even if we believe we're fundamentally worthless, reaching the goals we've tied our self-worth to can still produce feelings of tethered self-worth. This may seem surprising. At first glance, it might appear that tethered self-worth and a sense of worthlessness can't coexist. In reality, they often do. We can hold conflicting emotions about our personal value at the same time.

The feelings of tethered self-worth we generate by reaching these objectives can actually "protect" our conscious minds from the belief that we're fundamentally worthless. These feelings can *suppress* that underlying perception in the subconscious. However, if we don't meet these outcomes, we don't produce this "mental shield" of tethered self-worth. Without it, the belief and feeling of being inherently worthless can rise into conscious awareness. It's also worth noting that tethered self-worth isn't always effective at keeping this perception buried. Even when we get results that briefly boost our sense of value, a deep belief in our worthlessness can still surface.

What happened to our instinctive self-esteem as we grew up? It never actually went away — we all still have it. Our instinctive self-value wasn't erased by the belief or feeling that we're intrinsically worthless. As mentioned earlier, different emotions about our personal value can exist side by side. Instinctive self-worth is something we generate automatically. It isn't shaped by our thoughts or beliefs about ourselves, which is why it remains untouched by the idea that we lack inner value. And it's for this reason that it stays with us throughout our lives.

The reason we may not have consciously noticed our instinctive self-esteem during these times is that feelings of worthlessness are much "louder". Our innate self-value is still there. It's just hard to "hear" beneath all the "noise" created by those overpowering beliefs. We also may not have thought to look for these feelings, simply because we weren't aware they existed. That said, I think most of us have in difficult times tapped into a quiet, instinctive self-worth and found strength in it. Even without comprehending exactly where it came from. Once we consciously recognize that these instinctive feelings exist, they become much easier to find.

How We Challenge the Belief We Have No Intrinsic Worth

The ideal step at this point is to dismantle the self-perception that we're fundamentally worthless. When we break the logic behind this belief, the emotions that come with it also fade. Once that happens, our instinctive self-esteem becomes easier to notice. From this place of emotional security, we can begin doing things for their own sake, not just to avoid the discomfort of feeling unworthy.

So how do we stop believing that we're fundamentally worthless?

By recognizing that this idea persists *out of habit, not logic*. For it to be logical, there would need to be some evidence or reasoning behind it — but there isn't. It stays with us simply because it's been reinforced over time and conditioned into us. In fact, there's no logic to break, because none was there to begin with. When we assume a belief is logical, it becomes harder to question. But when we allow for the possibility that it exists purely out of habit, it becomes much easier to challenge.

It's important to understand that we don't need to be deserving of personal value. *We already have it*, in the form of instinctive self-worth. We generated it as children and continue to do so as adults. It's always there. This instinctive self-worth forms the *foundation of our self-esteem*. It's a kind of self-esteem that doesn't depend on what happens to us. When we dismantle the belief that we're worthless, we're not "getting our self-worth back" as if it had disappeared. We're simply making it easier to hear something that has always been present, and always will be.

Although we may have unlearned the belief that we have no intrinsic worth, we need to stay mindful not to fall back into the habit of believing it again. But if we do find ourselves adopting it again in the future, it should be easier to let go of, since we now understand how to break it.

Once we've discarded the notion that any belief in our fundamental worthlessness is logical, will we continue tying our self-value to outcomes? I think it depends on the individual, but for the most part, no. Once we recognize our innate self-worth as the foundation of self-esteem, that alone tends to be enough. We don't need to grow our sense of worth further. Personally, I don't want my sense of value to be shaped or influenced by external things. I do not want my ability to attain objectives to be a measure of my self-regard. I like the idea that the instinctive self-esteem I already have is enough.

Not tying my personal value to outcomes also helps me engage more deeply with the task itself. When I approach it with this mindset, I'm not thinking about how it might boost my self-esteem. I'm simply absorbed in the details of each moment. I like that I'm not doing this to "prove myself", but because I genuinely enjoy the experience and find it interesting. And as I continue with this activity, I keep building skills in this space, allowing me to create even more rewarding experiences from it.

How Aiming to Be Someone We Like and Respect Can Increase Our Self-Worth

To be someone we like and respect, we need to act in line with our conscience — that is, with our sense of right and wrong. When we don't, it becomes much harder to genuinely like and respect ourselves.

Aiming to be someone we like and respect can also increase our self-worth. This is because we can't help but tie our self-esteem to the outcome of us doing the right thing. So when we act in line with our values, we not only like and respect ourselves more, we also generate feelings of tethered self-worth. These feelings build on top of the innate self-esteem we always carry. However, when we do the wrong thing, we find it harder to like and respect ourselves, and we generate dissatisfying feelings of low self-worth. These feelings of being low also sit on top of our instinctive self-esteem. These distressing emotions can make it harder to "hear" our innate self-worth.

In my view, it is not possible to untether our self-esteem from doing the right thing. So if we want to strengthen our sense of personal value and make it easier to "hear" what's innate, we should aim to be someone we genuinely like and respect. That means acting in line with our conscience and striving to do what we believe is right.

To be clear, striving to like and respect myself doesn't mean I have to feel that way about every part of me. There are traits I consider undesirable — like the impulse to act against my conscience — that I don't want to like or respect. Still, I don't hate those parts of myself either. That kind of self-hatred isn't helpful. Instead, I aim to understand where those traits come from. By recognizing why I have the impulse to do the wrong thing, I can better manage it and increase the chances of acting in line with my conscience. Rather than dwell in unconstructive self-hatred, I try to *accept and make peace with the parts of myself I find undesirable*, all while working to improve them.

Everyone should aim to like, respect, and be at peace with themselves. This not only strengthens our sense of self-worth, but also makes it easier to enter a happy mental state. It helps us feel self-love more easily as well.

HOW TO STOP OUR EGO FROM CREATING ANGER

In Chapter 1, we explored how the ego's worry about appearing foolish could diminish our enjoyment of an activity. In this chapter, we'll examine a different worry it has that should also have its logic broken: *that we lack the kinds of power it cares about.* The ego's unease over this can lead to emotional suffering in the form of anger. We'll now examine how this kind of anger stems from this attachment to power.

At its most basic level, "power" can be defined as the ability to change something or to prevent it from being changed. We can identify different forms by considering the various things we might want to influence or protect from change. Common examples include financial influence, social dominance, economic control, and physical strength. There are a lot more.

When our ego is attached to particular forms of power, it scans our memories for times when we had that control — and when we didn't. If it finds a memory where we lacked the influence it values, it can trigger feelings of powerlessness and helplessness. These are not feelings of *complete* powerlessness or helplessness, but are specifically tied to the kind of power we lacked and the particular memory involved. In response to these distressing emotions, we can produce feelings of anger. This anger can be highly associated with the memory, so that whenever we recall that memory, we recall the anger as well.

When we feel angry about an event, we usually assume the event itself caused the anger. In my view, while the event plays a role, it's not the main cause. The deeper cause is the ego's attachment to particular forms of power, which leads us to respond with feelings of powerlessness, helplessness, and anger. If the same event happened to someone whose ego wasn't invested in those forms of control, they likely wouldn't feel the same emotional distress. They could more easily find peace with the event and move on. Their relationship with the memory would be one of peace, not anger.

It's because our ego is so attached to these types of power that some memories carry so much anger. These angry memories can often pull our attention away from the present and back into the past. In other words, ego-driven anger can regularly interfere with our ability to enter the playful mind in our current endeavors. Someone whose ego isn't tied to these forms of control doesn't experience this kind of interference with their happiness and enjoyment.

Is There a Benefit to Letting Our Ego Be Attached to Power?

Some people might think we're better off letting the ego cling to these power types. They see the ego's caring and hurting as a necessary emotional driver for getting what they want. They assume that without the ego behaving this way, they'd lose the motivation to pursue their goals. But this is a mistaken assumption. Even without the ego's involvement, we would still feel drawn to pursue what we want. After all, we desire interesting and engaging experiences that satisfy us. We would still take action, but no longer out of a need to frame ourselves as "having power" or to "feel powerful".

So our ego caring and hurting may not be necessary for attaining our interests. But does it make us better at doing so? While there may be situations where it seems to help, I believe it generally doesn't. If anything, it tends to get in the way. To get what we want, we usually need to think clearly about the obstacles in front of us, identify the solution, and carry it out. But feelings like powerlessness, helplessness, and anger can disrupt our thinking at any stage of that process, making it harder to succeed. It's obviously more useful to approach things with a clear head.

Given the above, it seems sensible to reduce the number of power types our ego cares about having, as it will reduce the anger we carry with us in our memories. This, in turn, will improve our ability to experience happiness and contentment in the present.

How Do We Convince Our Ego to Care About Fewer Power Types?

To begin with, the ego needs to recognize that it's logistically impossible for any individual to possess every conceivable form of power. No one can be powerful in all ways. If the ego clings to having all types of control in every situation, it will experience a great deal of anger. This is because it will constantly encounter situations where it lacks that power. A person with such an ego will end up carrying far more anger in their memories. Finding peace, moving on, and feeling happy will be much more difficult.

If we can't have all types of power, then our ego needs to *prioritize* which ones to care about and which to let go of based on their importance. If it's going to get upset over lacking control, it should at least be over something that genuinely matters to us, not over forms of influence that are relatively unimportant.

How do we determine which forms of control truly matter? It can be tricky, but I believe it's often clear which one stands out above the rest. There's usually one we want more than any other, which is the kind we care about most, deep down. *It's the ability to shape our own emotional state.* It's the ability to influence our own happiness and satisfaction. In my view, this rises well above the rest in importance.

The irony is that what *most disrupts* our ability to govern our emotional state is the ego's attachment to other, less important forms of control. When it notices we lack these, it triggers anger, which then disrupts our ability to enter the playful mind. As a result, we lose access to the happiness and deeper contentment we could have experienced by simply being open and engaged with what we're doing. In other words, by clinging to these relatively unimportant forms of control, the ego ends up sacrificing the one that matters most to it. It actively interferes with its own core aim, trading what it values most for something of far less importance. To protect this power over our emotional state, our ego has to detach itself from these less important power types. When the ego grasps this trade-off, we break the very logic that made it cling to these less important forms of control in the first place.

Our ego may struggle to let go of these less important forms of control because it fears looking foolish to others. But we can ease this fear by recognizing that, deep down, everyone wants to free themselves in the same way; at our core, we all want to be happy. And it's much easier to be happy when we're able to find peace and move on from past events. That becomes difficult when the ego clings to these lesser forms of control and suffers because of them. In short, people want to let go of these lesser attachments because they keep getting in the way of happiness. It would actually be the greater fool who continues letting ourselves suffer needlessly over these things.

There are two things worth clarifying about what we've discussed so far.

Firstly, we have not eliminated the ego. It is still there. What we've done is break the logic that made it cling to less important kinds of power. As a result, the ego now has much less ability to cause distress in the form of anger. Its emotional influence over us has been greatly reduced. We're much less mentally susceptible to suffer in this way going forward.

Secondly, we have not eliminated the underlying memory of the undesirable event. That is also still there. We've just made it so that we don't respond to that memory with egotistic feelings of powerlessness, helplessness, and anger. We've replaced them with feelings of peace.

It might be tempting to *hate* the ego, since it seems to cause so much of our pain. However, that hatred only adds another layer of suffering. Instead, it's better to accept it as part of us and make peace with it. This becomes easier once we've weakened its ability to influence our emotional state.

How to Keep the Ego from Reacting with Anger to Others' Actions

So far, we've discussed the main arguments for convincing the ego to let go of less important forms of power in general. Shortly, we'll turn to specific examples, focusing on two particular kinds of control, both involving our attempts to stop others from acting in ways we find undesirable.

The reason we're focusing on these types is that when the ego is attached to them, they tend to cause the most anger, *more than almost anything else*. Such attachments *interfere the most* with our power over our emotional state. By helping the ego detach from these forms of control, we can reduce the emotional distress we feel in response to others' actions without sacrificing the more important control we have over ourselves. Once this detachment is complete, there will be less interference with our happiness, and it will be easier to find peace with others' actions and move on.

Before we explore these two types, there are a few common assumptions in this area that need to be reconsidered.

The first assumption is that any feelings of powerlessness, helplessness, or anger we experience in response to someone's undesirable action are *primarily caused* by that action itself. In other words, we tend to believe that the other person's behavior is the main source of any emotional distress we experience.

This assumption is incorrect. The primary cause of these distressing emotions is not the action itself, but *our ego's response to the action*. To be more precise, the primary cause is our ego's attachment to having control over preventing the undesirable action. The *more* types of control the ego is attached to in relation to stopping the action, the *more* it generates feelings of powerlessness, helplessness, and anger. If the same action were directed at someone whose ego was more detached, they would not experience the same emotional distress. They would have avoided that unnecessary suffering and remained more at peace.

Since our ego is the cause of our distress, any feelings of powerlessness, helplessness, or anger we experience in response are ultimately self-inflicted. We are the ones making ourselves feel this way. It is not the other person's action that is hurting us, but our own mind turning against itself. *It has always been the mind hurting itself. It's impossible for anyone other than ourselves to cause us emotional suffering.* By contrast, a mind whose ego is detached from these forms of control will not inflict such anguish on itself.

When we mistakenly assume that someone else is the primary cause of our emotional distress, we also frame them more specifically as having exerted power over our emotional state. But since our ego is the actual cause, it means that whenever we experience powerlessness, helplessness, or anger, we are the ones exercising power over our emotional state — not the other person. It has always been us wielding that control over ourselves. It was never anyone else. We simply didn't understand how to use this power in a way that avoids self-inflicted pain. We didn't see how to help the ego stop clinging to so many unimportant concerns. And one major reason we failed to manage this inner influence effectively is that we weren't even aware we had it.

The second assumption we often make is that the other person has "made us" or "changed us" into someone who suffers emotionally because of their undesirable action. As if we had no capacity for suffering until they did something that transformed us into this state. But this is also incorrect. Even before they acted, we already had a mental vulnerability to suffer because our ego was already conditioned to fixate on these forms of control. It was already primed to respond with distress.

The other person didn't "make us" or "change us" into anything. They didn't create the ego. They didn't create the part of us that feels powerless, helpless, or angry. That was already part of us. If the ego were detached from these forms of control, we wouldn't have that vulnerability to begin with.

Put simply, if I find myself suffering emotionally in response to someone's action, I'd be less concerned about what they did and more focused on what within me created the vulnerability to suffer in the first place. Another way to frame it: I'd worry less about why my castle is being attacked, and more about why it doesn't have any defenses.

The main reason we're questioning these assumptions is that they *add* to the emotional suffering we're already experiencing. For instance, we may already feel powerlessness, helplessness, and anger because our ego is strongly attached to these forms of control. But if we also believe that the other person is the primary cause of this distress, that belief can create even more of the same emotions. The idea that someone else is responsible for our suffering can, in itself, make us suffer further. By letting go of these assumptions, we remove this added layer of distress.

Another reason we challenge these assumptions is that the ego won't let go of these forms of control if it still sees the other person as the primary cause of our pain. It becomes much easier for the ego to release these attachments once the assumptions that misattribute blame are no longer in place.

THE POWER TO STOP OTHERS FROM TREATING US WRONGLY

When the ego is attached to having the power to stop someone from doing something wrong to us, it reacts to that action with emotional distress. That reaction is in the form of powerlessness, helplessness, and anger. But this response is unnecessary. A person whose ego is not attached to this kind of control wouldn't experience those emotions. Yes, the action may be wrong, but we don't have to suffer because of it.

So how do we convince our ego to detach from this control?

Our ego may hesitate to let go of the power to prevent others' wrong actions if it believes we *inevitably suffer* as a result. But this hesitation should fade once we recognize that it's not the action itself, but the ego that creates the emotional pain that usually follows. We can avoid generating these distressing emotions by helping the ego release its attachment to this form of control.

Simply recognizing this may not be enough to get the ego to stop caring. It needs to see that the power to prevent someone else's wrong action is *relatively unimportant* compared to the power we have over our own emotional state. As discussed, this is the form of control we value most. After all, it's the influence over our happiness and satisfaction. The ego must come to see that clinging to this lesser control leads to emotional distress, which then *disrupts* our ability to control our mental state. It goes against the ego's own logic to care about a lesser power when it undermines a greater one, especially the one that matters most.

It's also illogical for the ego to care so deeply about the power to prevent others from doing wrong by us, given that it's physically impossible to go through life without this happening at some point. It is the cost of doing business, but should we allow ourselves to suffer in response *every single time it happens*? That's a lot of suffering to carry around in our memories — and most of it is unnecessary. No matter what we do, our interests will always be vulnerable in some way to the wrongful actions of others. While we can take steps to reduce that vulnerability, we can't eliminate it entirely.

While our interests may always remain vulnerable in some way to outside interference, we can still ensure that we are not *emotionally vulnerable* when those interests are affected by the wrong actions of others. We do this by getting our ego to detach from this power. When this change takes place, another person's wrong action might impact our interests, but it won't disturb our happiness.

Why the Ego May Struggle to Let Go of This Power

The ego may struggle to let go of the power to prevent a wrong action if it believes that others have used that action to get closer to happiness. But in reality, it's more likely that such a person has harmed their emotional state more rather than helped it. When someone acts against their own sense of right and wrong — their conscience — they make it harder to like, respect, or be at peace with themselves. And when someone feels this way about themselves, happiness becomes much harder to attain. Their actions also tend to generate feelings like disappointment, shame, and self-hatred. This emotional turmoil further disrupts their ability to be happy. Rather than moving closer to happiness, doing the wrong thing actually *pushes it further out of reach.*

It is useful for us to understand why a person would even think that doing such an action would bring them closer to happiness. When we see the "why", we realize that people often do the wrong thing because they have a *poor understanding of themselves* and of what actually brings them happiness. After seeing such a person in this light, it becomes very difficult for our ego to regard them as having any power over their own happiness.

Two False Beliefs That Drive Immoral Behavior

There are two ways in which people think doing a wrong action will get them closer to happiness.

The first is that they perceive some kind of "benefit" they believe they'll gain by doing the wrong thing — and assume that benefit is connected to happiness. For example, someone might commit theft to obtain a watch, thinking it will make them happier. They've been conditioned to believe there's a causal link between that benefit and genuine satisfaction. But what they often find is that, even after getting what they wanted, they don't feel much better deep down. They're still not happy. If they had a deeper understanding of themselves, they'd recognize that the benefit has little to do with happiness, and consequently, they would feel far less inclined to take that path.

The second way people believe a wrong action will bring them closer to happiness is when they're experiencing emotional suffering and want to take it out on someone else. Another person may have wronged them, and their ego responds with feelings of powerlessness, helplessness, and anger. They believe such distress inside of them has been created by this other person, so they want to create these same emotions in another. They believe rather desperately that their own emotional pain will disappear if they get others to experience the same thing. They think that with this hurt gone, they will get closer to happiness.

But when they act on this impulse and take their suffering out on others, they find that it doesn't work. The pain doesn't go away. It doesn't help them manage or eliminate their distress. The hurt remains, and they're no closer to happiness. If they understood themselves better, they'd recognize that the actual cause of their emotional pain is the ego's attachment to particular forms of control. They'd see that lashing out isn't a sign of power, but a response to the emotional suffering they've created within themselves. It's the action of someone struggling to cope with their own helplessness. They'd also realize that the solution lies in helping the ego let go of these attachments. Only those who *learn how to manage the ego* move closer to happiness. Such people don't let their actions be shaped by ego-driven suffering.

The Role of Self-Deception in Immoral Behavior

It becomes even harder to see someone who behaves immorally as having any power over their happiness once we recognize *how easily they deceive themselves*. Often, when a person does something wrong, they must convince themselves that their action isn't in conflict with their conscience. This self-deception helps them ignore their inner sense of right and wrong, making it easier to carry out the action. It allows them to pursue the benefit or take out their pain on someone else with less internal resistance.

However, this self-deception operates only in the conscious mind — not in the subconscious. While they may consciously believe the action isn't wrong, their subconscious is fully aware that it is. The subconscious isn't fooled. So even if they convince themselves on the surface, the wrong action still makes it harder for them to like, respect, and be at peace with themselves. They still push happiness further out of reach. They still feel disappointment, shame, and self-hatred. Self-deception doesn't protect a person from the emotional consequences of acting against their conscience. Even after the action is done, they may continue to believe it wasn't wrong, but the emotional cost remains.

Without consciously recognizing that their action was wrong, it becomes difficult for them to change their future behavior in ways that align with their conscience. In other words, they will continue acting in ways that make it harder to like, respect, and be at peace with themselves. This is why, when we see how easily someone like this deceives themselves, it becomes even harder to view them as having any control over their happiness. A person who deceives themselves lacks the ability to solve the problem of unhappiness.

By contrast, those who feel the impulse to do the wrong thing but choose not to act on it are able to do so because they're *honest with themselves*. They recognize that the action they're considering goes against their conscience. As a result, they can more clearly see that acting against their own sense of right and wrong isn't worth the cost of making it harder to like, respect, and be at peace with themselves. They understand that rather than bringing them closer to happiness, the action would only push it further away. A person who is honest with themselves in this way has far more control over their happiness than someone who is not.

When we look at someone who does the wrong thing, it often comes down to ignorance: ignorance of themselves and of what actually leads to happiness. It's a lack of understanding about how to manage their ego and how to stop their actions from being driven by the suffering they've created within. They're unaware of how essential self-honesty is to sustaining happiness, and how deeply self-deception undermines it. Without this awareness, it becomes much harder for them to do what's right and act in line with their conscience. And if they weren't so confused about what actually brings happiness, it would be far easier for them to act in ways that create it.

The Role of Luck in Developing Moral Awareness

What determines whether someone is aware or unaware of the impact that behaving immorally has on their happiness? Those who understand this often gain that insight from the people who surrounded them growing up, or they manage to figure it out on their own by observing how their actions affect their emotional state. Whether we develop this kind of self-awareness is largely a *matter of luck*. It's luck if we happen to grow up around the right people. It's chance if we happen to be the kind of person who can figure it out for ourselves. And it's also chance if we end up ignorant, because we had neither the right influences nor the capacity to see it clearly on our own. When I think about someone who behaves immorally, I think about how they *didn't choose* the people they were surrounded by growing up. I think about how they *didn't choose* to be the kind of person who couldn't figure it out for themselves. It was all luck.

I'm not saying all this because I think we should stop holding people accountable for acting unethically. As a practical matter, accountability is necessary. People need to face consequences as a *deterrent* to such behavior. I'm also not suggesting that we must be compassionate or forgiving toward them. This isn't about them. It's about us. It's about doing what's best for our own happiness. And that means letting go of anger.

It can become easier to release that anger when we recognize that the person who did the wrong thing acted out of ignorance. An ignorance that, at its core, wasn't something they chose. It's the kind of ignorance that will keep pushing happiness further out of their reach. When our anger fades, we find it easier to make peace with what happened and move on. Letting go of anger is necessary for our peace of mind, but it doesn't require us to feel compassion or offer forgiveness. If anything, once we see the depth of their ignorance, our feelings may settle somewhere between indifference and pity.

We should appreciate how lucky we are that we didn't turn out like this other person, especially considering how easily we could have. We *happened* to develop enough self-understanding, and enough clarity about what makes us happy, to generally choose the right path. But if we had been born into the same circumstances and lived the same life as the person who wronged us, we likely wouldn't have developed that same self-awareness.

We should also keep in mind that while this person may have treated us poorly, they may have previously experienced something far worse at the hands of someone else. When we consider this — and recognize that they haven't learned how to manage their ego — it becomes easier to understand how their actions are being driven by ego-based pain. We should be grateful that our sense of right and wrong has not been warped like theirs. We should be glad that we don't think like they do. We should appreciate that, to the extent that we've had wrong done by us, we've learned how to manage our ego, find peace, move on, and be happy.

Helping Someone Understand Themselves so They Act Less Immorally

Recognizing that ignorance is what enables someone to do the wrong thing is valuable, as it puts us in the best position to prevent such actions in the future. We can reduce their incentive to behave this way by helping them better understand themselves and what actually leads to happiness. In doing so, we help clear away the confusion and false beliefs driving their behavior.

This might involve showing them that there's no real connection between the perceived benefit of a wrong action and lasting happiness. Stealing from others or betraying their trust doesn't make them genuinely satisfied. It might also mean helping them see that taking out their emotional pain on others doesn't relieve it. Most importantly, they need to understand that behaving immorally ultimately undermines their deeper goal of being happy. In that it makes it harder for them to like, respect, and be at peace with themselves. They need to see that the way they're pursuing happiness simply doesn't work.

If they're someone who feels powerless, helpless, and angry

because of their ego, we can help them learn how to let go of that pain so they don't take it out on others. After all, we've all had to manage our own egos in similar ways. We've all been there. We can show them that suffering isn't an inevitable response to the wrong actions of others. We can help them learn how to guide their ego to detach from these less important forms of control. In doing so, we assist them in what they've truly wanted all along: let go, find peace, and feel good again.

When trying to have this conversation with someone, they may be deceiving themselves into thinking that what they're considering isn't wrong. As mentioned earlier, this self-deception operates in their conscious mind, but not in their subconscious. Deep down, they're aware that what they're thinking of doing goes against their conscience. Our goal, then, is to make it as difficult as possible for them to maintain that self-deception.

The Simplest Way to Challenge a Self-Deception

One of the simplest ways to challenge it is to apply a basic role-reversal test. This involves asking: *would it be acceptable if someone else did the same thing to you?* An action should be wrong regardless of who does it. What is wrong for one should be wrong for all. And if they genuinely believe it's not immoral, then they shouldn't feel angry if the same action is done to them.

This person might at least acknowledge that the action is wrong under "ordinary circumstances". For example, they may generally view stealing or lying as immoral. But then they offer a "justification" that makes the action seem acceptable in this particular case. In their eyes, the specifics of the situation cancel out the wrongness of the act. They no longer see it as immoral, believing they have a "good reason". Now, I do think there are exceptional situations where a genuine justification can make an otherwise wrong action no longer wrong. Self-defense in the case of killing is a clear example. But does this person honestly believe that this is one of those instances? Or is it just a self-deception? Is it simply a way to ignore their conscience while they take the benefit or take out their pain on another?

The simplest way to tell whether someone genuinely believes their "justification" — or is deceiving themselves — is to use a variation of the earlier role-reversal test. This means asking them: *would it be acceptable if someone else did the same thing to you for the same reason?* If they truly believe the justification cancels out the wrongness of the action, then they shouldn't object to someone else doing the same thing to them using the same reasoning. Can someone else steal from them, or lie to them, with the same rationale? If the answer is no — if they would feel wronged or angry — then it's likely that their reasoning is not sincere, but a form of self-deception.

It can't be that the same rationale makes an action acceptable for one person but not for another. Once again, what is wrong for one is wrong for all. This is a simple test that most justifications fail. People often claim they're justified in doing something wrong, yet become angry when someone else does the same thing to them, using the same explanation. They still see the other person's action as wrong, even though it's based on the very reasoning they used themselves.

When someone goes to such lengths to deceive themselves, it becomes difficult to respect them. There's something deeply unsteady about a person so desperate to avoid facing their own conscience that they fill their own mind with fabrications. Whatever lies they tell others, they pale in comparison to the ones they live by. In the end, the greatest fool they make is of themselves.

THE POWER TO GET JUST OUTCOMES WHEN ANOTHER TREATS US WRONGLY

We tend to speak of "injustice" when someone wrongs us and we don't receive a just outcome in response. By contrast, we consider "justice" to be present when those fair or appropriate outcomes have been attained.

In response to an injustice done to us, we may experience feelings of anger. This anger can arise from two different parts of us:

- One is the ego, which becomes upset about not having the power to secure just outcomes for itself. Alongside anger, this also evokes powerlessness and helplessness.
- The other is our *impartial* sense of justice, which can become angry regardless of whether it is we or someone else who is treated wrongly and has not gotten a just outcome. This reflects the non-egotistic side of us.

How Much of Our Anger Is Ego-Driven?

When an injustice is done to us, what *proportion of the anger* we feel in response comes from our ego, and how much comes from our impartial sense of justice?

One simple way to tell is to ask ourselves how angry we would feel if the same injustice were done to a complete stranger. For example, do we feel just as angry when someone gets away with stealing from or lying to another person as we do when we're the ones being wronged? While we may be upset in both cases, we tend to feel significantly more anger when the injustice is directed at us personally. This suggests that *most of our anger* is driven by the ego, with only a small portion coming from our impartial sense of justice.

Another question we can ask ourselves is how angry we get when we imagine *an even worse injustice* happening to a complete stranger. In most cases, we find ourselves far more upset by a relatively minor injustice done to us than by a more serious one done to someone else. For example, we may feel much angrier when someone steals from or lies to us than when we hear about a stranger being violently attacked. These kinds of questions reveal how strongly our ego influences us by making us care far more about the injustices we experience than those experienced by others.

In my view, it's actually a good thing that this anger comes almost entirely from our ego. That's because the ego can be managed. We can work with it so that it stops producing anger in response to not getting just outcomes. In other words, we have much more control over this kind of anger and can reduce or even eliminate it. We do this by helping the ego let go of its attachment to having the power to secure those outcomes. As a result, not only does the anger diminish, but so do the accompanying feelings of powerlessness and helplessness. By contrast, it's not as clear how to control the anger that comes from the impartial side of us.

Why Managing Ego Anger Makes Us More Effective at Getting Justice

Some people might worry that without the ego's fixation on justice — and the anger it produces — they won't feel motivated to pursue just outcomes. But this isn't the case. What we're doing here is simply addressing the ego's tendency to become emotionally attached to not getting justice. We can then be free of the powerlessness, helplessness, and anger that come from that attachment. We're not doing anything to stop our impartial sense of justice from caring. And because it does care, it still provides us with *resolve and some anger* that can fuel our efforts to pursue justice.

When we let our ego fixate on getting just outcomes, we end up pursuing justice from a place of emotional pain — one marked by powerlessness, helplessness, and anger. In this state, the drive for justice is primarily about easing our ego's distress. In other words, *our suffering ends up controlling our pursuit of justice.* But when we help the ego detach, our desire for justice is guided by impartiality instead. It comes from a place of calm resolve and a genuine belief in what is right. It does not come from egotistic hatred or a desperate need to relieve emotional pain.

But do we have more drive to pursue justice if we let our ego keep obsessing and fueling anger? I would say yes — we might feel more driven — but that doesn't mean we'd be more effective in actually attaining just outcomes. Excessive anger can easily become counterproductive. While some situations may call for aggression, in my view, most require level-headedness and less ego. When we lean more on our impartial sense of justice, we can still be assertive and firm without being aggressive. Many situations also demand nuanced thinking to reach justice. These situations are often complex and call for precision and clarity; both of which are hard to access when we're overwhelmed by anger. Otherwise, the consequences we administer may be disproportionate to the original wrongdoing, or we may harm innocent people who weren't responsible. In other words, justice turns into vengeance.

So for me, it's not worth allowing our ego to keep caring and being this angry since it overall hinders our ability to get justice. There's little value in being more driven if we lack the mental clarity to find the right solution. That's why I think we're generally more effective at securing just outcomes when we're not burdened by egotistic anger. Some people think it's foolish to stop the ego from caring about the power to get justice. But given how much it hinders this objective, it's actually more foolish to let it continue. When we rely on our impartial sense of justice instead, we can still be motivated without bringing in the counterproductive effects that come with ego-driven emotion. As mentioned, the impartial side of us can still create some anger, but it is not enough to make us suffer or be a hindrance.

Understanding the Different Forms of Justice That Exist

Recognizing all this may still not be enough to convince our ego to detach from the power to get justice. If that's the case, our ego will continue to feel anger in response to an injustice done to us. To further help our ego let go, we need to better understand what it sees as "just outcomes". We need to examine more closely what it's actually angry about not having. For most of us, our egos tend to define justice as the other person being held *accountable for their behavior* and *facing some kind of punishment*. Often, we take this to mean publicly exposing the person and ensuring they experience something unpleasant, ideally something that causes emotional suffering.

This is the more conventional form of justice — but it's not the only kind that exists. Just outcomes also include the *emotional consequences* a person faces when they act against their own conscience. By doing something they genuinely believe to be wrong, they make it harder to like, respect, and be at peace with themselves. Their actions take them farther from their fundamental goal of happiness instead of closer. They may feel disappointment, shame, and self-hatred. No amount of self-deception at the conscious level can stop the subconscious from holding them accountable. After all, they've violated their own sense of right and wrong. In this form of justice, the person is still being held accountable — psychologically — and still being punished.

The only way for such a person to alleviate these emotional effects of doing the wrong thing is *honest self-reflection in their conscious mind*. This means *consciously accepting* that they acted against their own sense of right and wrong, and holding themselves accountable not just at a subconscious level, but consciously as well. Doing so can lessen the emotional turmoil to some extent, often replacing it with feelings of contrition. But to find deeper relief, restore peace, and truly move on, they will need to go further. They will need to make amends. By contrast, if they avoid this self-honesty and continue deceiving themselves into thinking their action wasn't wrong, they won't escape these emotional consequences. They will struggle to genuinely like, respect, or be at peace with themselves. While they might evade more conventional forms of justice, they cannot avoid the kind that arises through their deteriorated emotional state.

Though we may not secure conventional justice, another form remains active, one that arguably harms the other person's happiness even more. Ironically, when we hold them accountable and prompt honest self-reflection, we're actually helping them move closer to peace, closure, and genuine contentment. But by evading conventional justice and self-reflection, they also evade the very solution to the suffering they've caused themselves by behaving immorally. Their avoidance sabotages their fundamental goal of happiness.

Also consider that when people behave immorally, it's often because they're already unhappy. They believe the action will bring them a benefit they associate with genuine satisfaction, or they're trying to relieve their pain by taking it out on someone else. They think this will make them feel better, when in reality, it only sabotages their well-being. Helping such individuals face conventional just outcomes and engage in honest self-reflection can begin to undo their mistaken beliefs about what really leads to happiness. From there, they can start acting in ways that genuinely support their emotional well-being. But this change won't happen if they continue avoiding accountability and self-honesty.

Much of our ego's anger over not getting conventional just outcomes stems from the assumption that no justice has occurred at all. But this assumption is incorrect, and recognizing that can significantly reduce the anger. There *are* still just outcomes in the form of emotional consequences. The person who acted immorally is still being held to account, as genuine happiness becomes harder for them to attain. And happiness, arguably, is the most important thing to them — the very reason they took the action in the first place.

They cannot escape justice entirely. No matter what they do, some form of accountability remains. That said, emotional consequences are not a replacement for conventional justice. We should still strive to pursue conventional just outcomes wherever possible. But there will be times when that kind of justice simply isn't practical or exceedingly difficult to attain. In those cases, while we may not get the outcome we *prefer*, we can at least recognize that justice exists in another form. Whatever it is, we should not allow ourselves to suffer if we don't get our preference.

No Longer Tying Our Happiness to Another's Suffering

Reducing the ego's anger in this way has not involved detaching it from the power to secure just outcomes. The ego still clings to this power, but it no longer gets angry because it recognizes that the other person cannot completely escape justice. Even if conventional justice isn't attained, justice still exists in the form of emotional consequences. But this approach ties our happiness, to some extent, to the other person's emotional suffering. For the ego to remain calm and not interfere with our happiness, it needs to believe they're hurting inside.

Personally, I don't like having my happiness depend in any way on whether the other person suffers or repents. I want to feel just as happy regardless of what happens to them. More fundamentally, I don't want to be the kind of person who needs to think of someone else suffering just to quiet my ego's anger. To remove this dependency, I have to convince my ego to let go of its attachment to getting just outcomes altogether. Even as my ego releases this need, my impartial side will still care about justice. I can rely primarily on its quiet resolve to motivate me in pursuing conventional justice.

How do we convince the ego to let go of its attachment to getting just outcomes altogether, so that we can finally free our happiness from depending on whether the other person suffers?

The ego can detach from the need for justice when it realizes that the *ultimate just outcome* is this: our happiness remains unaffected by the wrongdoing and is entirely independent of the other person's fate. In other words, if the ego genuinely wants the highest form of justice, it must not care about the power to get just outcomes at all. In this way, we have broken the logic that makes the ego cling to this power. To be clear, attaining this ultimate outcome through ego detachment doesn't mean we stop pursuing conventional justice. Our impartial side still values that. And since these two forms of justice aren't interchangeable, we should aim for both where possible.

It helps our ego to detach from getting just outcomes when we see how doing so can help our friends and loved ones manage their own egos. Often, a person allows their ego to become attached to this power because they've observed those around them holding the same attachments. They've watched others tie their happiness to whether those who wronged them end up suffering. Surrounded by that mindset, they assume it's the only option. No one has shown them another way. But when we demonstrate that it's *possible* to let go, that we can detach our ego and keep our happiness independent of another person's pain, we offer them an alternative. We show them it's possible to find peace and move on without needing someone else to suffer.

When I think about specific injustices I've experienced, part of me wishes they had never happened — yet another part feels strangely grateful they did. I feel this way because those experiences allow me to support people I care about who have faced or may face similar injustices. Because this happened to me, I'm better positioned to help someone navigate their ego in response to it. Ideally, the injustice never happens to them, but I'm glad to have the ability to help if needed. They can see that they don't have to go it alone. They can be shown that it is possible — and acceptable — to move on.

By helping our ego let go of its obsession, we can also show others how to pursue just outcomes, not from ego, but from an impartial sense of justice. We can demonstrate how to act not out of powerlessness, helplessness, or anger, but from a place of steady resolve. We can show what it means to seek justice because it's right, not simply to soothe ego-driven pain. We should be teaching one another how to access this resolve, not how to inflame the ego.

HOW TO ALLEVIATE DESPAIR

There is a mental framework — unrelated to our self-worth or ego — that can give rise to emotional suffering in the form of despair. By breaking down this pattern of thinking, we reduce its power to generate such anguish.

This mental framework is what I call a "happiness conditional statement". It's the belief that our happiness depends on a specific condition being met: that it is impossible for us to be happy if a particular event happens or fails to happen. For instance, we might believe we can't be happy if someone treats us poorly. So when that mistreatment occurs, we respond with the belief that happiness is forever gone, which leads to despair. Another person could experience the same mistreatment, but because they don't believe happiness is permanently lost, they won't fall into despair. They might feel disappointed that the event occurred, but they wouldn't experience the deeper anguish of despair, which is much worse.

What this shows is that the despair isn't caused by the event itself, but by the belief that happiness is no longer possible. This emotional anguish is simply the mind inflicting suffering on itself. People who have adopted conditional beliefs about happiness often mistakenly assume that their despair is caused by the event. Once they realize that the anguish comes not from the event, but from the belief that happiness is out of reach, they become more willing to abandon that belief. As the happiness conditional statement dissolves, so does its power to cause suffering.

We may hold *multiple* happiness conditional statements. That is, we may believe there are several different events which, if any were to happen (or not happen), would make happiness feel impossible. Each of these happiness conditions has the potential to trigger despair. For this reason, we should aim to dismantle as many of them as we can. Most of these beliefs can be broken down using the same logic described earlier.

The main challenge in undoing these beliefs is that they can be difficult to identify. Many were subconsciously adopted as we were growing up, so we're often unaware that we hold them. When a triggering event occurs, we may feel despair without realizing it stems from one of these hidden conditions. In those moments, we tend to assume the despair is caused entirely by the event itself.

So far, we've dismantled what I believe is the most commonly held happiness conditional statement: the belief that we can't be happy because we've been treated wrongly. This is one of the most frequent sources of despair. Next, we'll look at how to break down a couple of other widely adopted conditional statements.

Statement #1: It Is Impossible to Be Happy While Emotionally Suffering

When we've adopted such a belief, we assume it's impossible to experience emotional suffering and happiness at the same time. So, whenever we detect any emotional distress within ourselves, we automatically conclude that there can't be any happiness or enjoyable feelings inside of us. We automatically think that all we are is hurt. Because we believe happiness is no longer possible, this adds a layer of despair on top of the pain we're already feeling.

I'm not sure why we assume emotional suffering can't exist alongside happiness or emotional satisfaction. After all, we're often distressed or dissatisfied about one thing while feeling happy or content about something else. Consider this example: you're at a restaurant with a friend. You may not enjoy the music playing, but you really like the food. Maybe you're still feeling glad about a recent promotion, yet also frustrated because you misplaced your wallet. In that moment, you're experiencing multiple emotional *triggers* — some creating satisfaction, others dissatisfaction — all at the same time:

- Music you're not in the mood for is creating emotional *dissatisfaction*.
- Food you like is creating emotional *satisfaction*.
- The thought that you have been promoted is creating emotional *satisfaction*.
- The thought that you have misplaced your wallet is creating emotional *dissatisfaction*.

As we can see, it's possible to simultaneously feel emotionally satisfied for some reasons and dissatisfied for others. So when we notice emotional suffering within us, we shouldn't assume that happiness or satisfaction is entirely absent. That distress reflects only part of our emotional state, not the whole. While suffering can make happiness harder to access, it doesn't make it impossible. When we accept that it's still possible to feel happy even while a part of us hurts, we've dismantled this particular happiness condition.

The benefit of this mindset is that when we notice emotional distress within ourselves, we don't respond to it with despair. We avoid unnecessarily adding to the hurt. This is why, as a general rule, no matter what situation we're in, it's always better to believe that happiness is still possible. It's often the belief that we can't be happy that keeps us from it.

The real danger of believing in this happiness condition is that even a small trace of emotional distress can be misinterpreted as the complete absence of happiness or satisfaction. This misinterpretation of our emotional state can itself push us into full despair. What began as a minor hurt is suddenly and unnecessarily amplified.

Statement #2: It Is Impossible to Be Happy When Not Getting What We Want

Up to this point, we've focused on beliefs that make happiness feel out of reach when unwanted events occur. Now, we'll turn to beliefs that make happiness seem impossible *unless* a specific desired event takes place. So, until this event happens, we believe we cannot be happy —and this leads to feelings of despair in the meantime. For example, we might adopt a happiness condition that says we can't be happy unless we land a particular job. As a result, we feel despair until we get it.

The way to break our belief in this happiness conditional statement is to recognize that this gloom isn't caused by the event not occurring. It's not caused by us not getting the job. Once again, it's caused by the belief that happiness is impossible. If we did not have this thought pattern, we may be disappointed by the event not happening, but we would not despair.

Also, we only think we need this event to be happy because we've been conditioned by those around us to believe so. We don't genuinely need it, we've simply *assumed* we do. The stronger this conditioning, the more time and effort it may take to let go of the belief.

BE MINDFUL OF OTHER HARMFUL FRAMEWORKS WE APPLY

In this chapter, we've explored how to dismantle frameworks related to self-worth, ego, and happiness conditional statements. All with the aim of reducing our mental vulnerability to suffering. If we still find ourselves experiencing emotional pain, it may be worth examining which patterns in our thinking are causing it.

There are a number of possibilities:

- If we're experiencing powerlessness, helplessness, or anger, it likely means our ego still values a form of power we haven't yet addressed.
- If we're feeling despair, it's probably due to a happiness conditional statement we haven't dismantled.
- If we're struggling with low self-worth, the likely cause is that we still believe — on some level — that we are fundamentally worthless, or that our value depends on attaining a goal we've yet to reach.
- If the emotional pain is of a different kind altogether, it may be rooted in a mental framework not covered in this book.

Many of these mental frameworks have been conditioned into us by the society we live in. Our ego, in particular, is taught to care about things that don't matter as much as we've been led to believe.

3

———

STOPPING OURSELVES FROM RECALLING UNWANTED MEMORIES

The primary reason we recall memories of undesirable events is that we apply mental frameworks to them that generate emotional pain. This distress pulls our attention away from the present and into the past. By dismantling these thought patterns — such as those tied to the ego or conditions we place on happiness — we eliminate the pain they produce. In doing so, we remove the main reason the memory resurfaces, making it easier to stay grounded in the here and now.

Even after we discard these frameworks and the pain subsides, we may still revisit the memory for other reasons. Though recalling it no longer hurts, that mental bandwidth could instead be spent on activities we find more engaging, useful, or satisfying. Pinpointing the mind's lingering motives is therefore helpful: once we understand them, we can usually challenge them. The fewer reasons the mind has to recall a memory, the less often it will resurface. When no reasons remain, it should stop appearing altogether.

One type of memory that's often recalled is when someone has wronged us. Even after we've dismantled the mental frameworks that once caused emotional suffering, the mind may still have reasons to bring the memory back. Below are the five most common ones.

REASON #1: WE THINK WE CAN LEARN USEFUL INFORMATION FROM A SURVIVAL PERSPECTIVE

When it comes to our survival, the mind may see two pieces of "useful information" to be gained from revisiting a memory:

- What steps can we take to prevent someone from doing this wrong action in the future? For example, how can we stop a close friend from betraying our trust?
- How can we avoid emotional suffering if the same action happens again? For instance, how do we prevent emotional anguish if someone we trust betrays us again?

As long as the mind believes there's something to be gained from revisiting a memory, it will keep bringing it up. Once it no longer sees any utility in the memory, it tends to recall it far less often.

As reasons go, this one isn't terrible. But we should recognize that there's a limit to how much useful information can be drawn from a memory. For example, we might learn something that *improves our chances* of preventing the action from happening again. Perhaps steps to physically stop someone from betraying us, or ways to persuade someone not to do it. But no memory can give us the ability to prevent the action with 100% certainty. If we don't recognize when we've likely extracted all the value it has to offer, we may keep revisiting it long after it's stopped being helpful. In my view, it doesn't take long to exhaust what a memory can teach us about preventing someone else's wrongdoing.

When it comes to learning how to avoid emotional distress if the action were to recur, how much useful information can we realistically draw from the memory? In most cases, quite a bit more. We can greatly reduce the likelihood of reacting with emotional pain to betrayal by identifying the specific mental frameworks behind our suffering. Once we've identified these patterns, we can begin breaking them, substantially lowering the risk of future distress.

Unfortunately, simply identifying and challenging these frameworks doesn't guarantee we'll never experience emotional suffering again. If the same wrong action happens again, we may slip back into those patterns without realizing it. That said, having learned about these frameworks should help us quickly recognize when we're relying on them. Once we're aware, we can begin unlearning them again. But if we insist on avoiding emotional distress with 100% certainty after betrayal, we'll keep revisiting the memory long after it has stopped being helpful. We need to accept that such certainty is impossible.

Even if we accept that we've likely reached the limit of useful insights a memory can offer, our survival instinct may still prompt us to revisit it. The push to recall can be driven by the mere *possibility* that something valuable might remain. This can happen even if the last several hundred recalls haven't revealed anything new about how to prevent betrayal or how to not suffer as a reaction to it. Of course, it's possible that some insight still lies undiscovered. We can never be certain. But it's equally possible that the memory has been fully mined for insight, and revisiting it offers no further benefit to our survival.

Once we've likely reached the limit of useful information, how do we stop the survival mind from wanting to recall the memory?

To begin with, we should recognize that even if some useful information remains, it's unlikely to *significantly* improve our chances of preventing the action or avoiding emotional distress. The more valuable insights about what we should do with respect to betrayal have already been extracted.

We should also consider how constantly recalling the memory may actually *hinder our survival* more than help it. While we're occupied with reliving the past, we risk becoming distracted from present tasks. Some of which could pose a physical danger if we're not paying attention. For example, while driving, we might be so focused on a memory of betrayal — trying to prevent something unlikely from happening — that we increase our risk of crashing, a far more likely danger. The time spent dwelling could instead be used for things that more directly improve our chances of survival, such as developing new skills or building social connections.

We'll now look at two key learnings our survival instinct seeks in order to prevent someone else's wrongdoing, and how we can gain that understanding without needing to constantly relive the memory.

Learning the Motivation Behind the Immoral Act

Identifying what motivates someone to act immorally can be key to preventing that behavior. Once we grasp their motivation, it might change how we respond. Either by adjusting the actions we take or by changing how we persuade them that acting unethically goes against their best interests. But how much of their motivation do we really need to understand in order to stop the behavior? The more deeply we think we need to understand it, the more likely we are to keep revisiting the memory.

In my view, we don't need to relive the memory to understand the core motivation behind most immoral actions. It's already quite clear. As discussed in the previous chapter, people often act unethically because they mistakenly believe it will bring them closer to happiness. They might see a benefit in the action — such as stealing a friend's wallet — and assume it will lead to genuine satisfaction. Or they may be in emotional pain and believe that taking it out on someone else will bring relief. Once we understand this core motivation, we can reduce their incentive to act immorally by helping them better understand themselves and what more likely brings happiness. When we recognize that this mistaken belief is what drives unethical behavior — and understand how to challenge it — there's much less reason to keep revisiting the memory.

To what extent should we relive a memory to understand the specific details of why someone acted the way they did? For example, we could learn more about what they believed they would gain from betraying a friend, or what past experiences led them to take out their emotional pain on others. In my view, we shouldn't think about this person any more than necessary. If we think there are still details that are absolutely *essential* for preventing the action, then it makes sense to keep recalling the memory. If, however, the details are somewhat helpful but *not essential* in stopping the behavior, I don't see a reason to investigate them.

Again, we can never learn enough to prevent the action with 100% certainty. If we aim for that, we risk staying stuck in the past with little useful information to show for it. Ultimately, how much valuable detail we can extract will vary from case to case.

Learning to Challenge Moral Self-Deception in Others

As mentioned in the previous chapter, someone who does the wrong thing is often deceiving themselves. They may subconsciously recognize that their actions go against their conscience, but consciously convince themselves that something like betraying a close friend isn't wrong. This self-deception makes it easier for them to follow through with the immoral action. We might feel tempted to revisit a memory in order to figure out how to break someone out of their self-deception and prevent another betrayal. If they are made to consciously acknowledge the action is wrong, it becomes more difficult for them to carry it out. We want to make it harder — if not impossible — for them to fool themselves.

We may recall our memories of this person to help us formulate logical arguments for why their action was immoral. If they offer rationalizations for their behavior, we search for logical ways to challenge them. For instance, they might claim that betraying a friend isn't wrong, or that they have a rationale that makes it acceptable.

Our ability to come up with logical arguments can go a long way in helping someone break out of self-deception, but it's not the ultimate determinant. A major reason people deceive themselves into thinking their action isn't immoral is to suppress the disappointment, shame, and self-hatred that arise from going against their conscience. To break through that self-deception — to consciously acknowledge the action as wrong — is to allow that emotional turmoil to surface in their awareness. Some people have the mental fortitude to face such uncomfortable, even painful, emotions. Those who can confront these feelings are the ones capable of breaking through the self-deception and admitting they acted wrongly.

But for those who *lack the mental fortitude* to tolerate such emotional distress, suppression becomes necessary. They must shield their conscious mind from the turmoil. This means deceiving themselves into believing they didn't do anything wrong. This "emotional interference" blocks their acknowledgment of immoral behavior, no matter the logical arguments put against them. To put it simply: breaking someone out of self-deception depends less on how logical we are, and more on how much mental and emotional strength the other person has.

If we're interested in breaking someone's self-deception, it's more effective to run the two role-reversal tests discussed in the previous chapter than to keep reliving the memory:

- If they genuinely believe, deep down, that the action isn't wrong, then they should have no issue with someone else doing the same thing to them.
- If they believe the action isn't wrong because they have a *justification*, then they should also be fine with someone else doing the same thing to them under the same justification.

Ultimately, if it isn't immoral for them to do something to others, then it shouldn't be considered immoral when the same thing is done to them. If they wouldn't be okay with being betrayed by someone they consider close, they're likely deceiving themselves into believing their own action wasn't wrong. These role-reversal tests spare us from having to capture all their reasoning, dissect it, or search for holes. They're the simplest and most effective way to prompt someone to acknowledge the immorality of their behavior.

However, whether these tests work still depends on the strength of the person's self-deception. If their mental fortitude is very weak, the tests may have little effect. This person might be too effective at suppressing the internal conflict and emotional turmoil. Though in many cases, that distress still surfaces consciously to some extent.

REASON #2: OUR EGO IS PUSHING US TO LEARN MORE FROM THE MEMORY

In some cases, it may not be our survival instinct pushing us to learn more from the memory, but our ego. The ego becomes anxious about appearing foolish to others if the same action happens again — whether by the same person or someone else — and tries to gather as much information as possible. The desperation to not look silly for being betrayed again can push the mind to keep revisiting the memory, even if it hasn't produced anything useful in a long time. The ego keeps searching anyway, even if we're aware that any new insight would only slightly improve our chances of preventing such an event.

The way to calm the ego's nervousness is to help it see that revisiting the memory beyond its point of usefulness is *even more foolish*. This realization can be arrived at in a number of ways.

Firstly, what if we go through life revisiting the memory of betrayal over and over, only to find we've been preparing for something that never happens again?

Secondly, even if we do gain useful information that helps prevent the wrong action in the future, was it really worth reliving that event in our minds so many times to get it? We may have avoided it happening again, but only after *mentally experiencing it thousands of times* anyway through frequent recall. Depending on the nature of the action, that might not be a trade-off worth making. In most cases, it's a foolish one.

Thirdly, instead of revisiting the memory, we could have spent that time engaged in activities that are far more satisfying, and frankly, much more interesting. We could have been developing skills or exploring rich conceptual spaces with far more depth and dimension. What the ego needs to honestly consider is the likelihood of the action happening again. If we're giving up these fulfilling experiences just to prepare for something unlikely, then we're playing the greater fool.

REASON #3: WE WANT TO GET CLOSURE ON THIS STORY

We may continue to relive a memory in search of closure, a state whereby we finally achieve a sense of resolution or emotional completion.

The problem is that we often expect *complete closure* — a full sense of resolution. But if we keep holding out for it, we may continue reliving the memory indefinitely, as that level of resolution is difficult to attain. If we want to move on from the past, we need to shift our expectations: instead of seeking complete closure, we focus on finding *sufficient* closure. This means reaching a sense of resolution that feels adequate on some level, even if not perfect. Because it's much easier to attain, sufficient closure makes it easier to stop reliving the memory.

We'll now look at several expectations where the desire for complete resolution is often unrealistic and may keep us stuck in the past. To move on, we need to adjust these expectations and aim for sufficient closure instead. Note that some of the things we want to understand from a survival perspective — to prevent the action — are the same things we seek from a closure perspective.

We Expect to Learn the Motivation Behind the Immoral Act

When we expect complete closure, we want to understand both their core motivation and every specific detail behind why they did it. This can take us beyond what's useful or necessary to prevent the action.

While the main reason may be clear, it's impossible to uncover every specific detail behind it. Our memory can only provide limited insight into what was going on in the other person's mind. If we expect to uncover every little detail, we may never stop reliving the memory.

Instead, we need to aim for a more realistic sense of resolution. In my view, it's often enough to understand the other person's core motivation and a *few* specific details. Full clarity isn't necessary to move on.

We Expect to Understand How Someone Could Not Recognize That Their Action Is Wrong

When we expect complete resolution in this area, we tend to relive the memory because we're trying to make sense of how someone could fail to see their behavior as immoral; especially when it seems so obvious to us that it is. How could they not be aware that violating someone's trust is wrong? We keep searching for the angle that allows them to avoid reaching that conclusion.

The explanation is usually straightforward: as mentioned earlier, the person is already subconsciously aware that what they did was wrong, but they're deceiving their conscious mind into thinking otherwise. That they acted unethically hasn't completely escaped their comprehension. They may even admit that the action — such as betraying someone's trust — is generally wrong, but claim that in this particular case, they had a "justification" that makes it acceptable. Yet deep down, they recognize this isn't true. After all, if someone did the same thing to them with the same reasoning, they'd see it as wrong. This kind of "justification" is usually just part of the self-deception.

In other words, we can't make sense of their reasoning because it doesn't actually make sense to them either. They have to consciously deceive themselves into believing it does. Once we see that the other person is already subconsciously *convinced* they acted unethically — and that their conscious reasoning is a product of self-deception that doesn't even make sense to them — that insight can provide sufficient closure.

We Expect to Learn How to Break Someone Out of Their Moral Self-Deception

Once we recognize that someone is subconsciously aware they acted immorally but is consciously deceiving themselves, we might expect that we can break through that denial. We come up with logical arguments in the hope that they'll acknowledge what they did was wrong and admit they had no valid excuse.

In our minds, we're not coming up with these arguments to convince them that what they did was wrong — deep down, they're already aware of that. Instead, we're trying to get them to consciously accept what their subconscious is already convinced of. To do this, we may find ourselves revisiting the memory in search of arguments that might break through their self-deception.

In such cases, we need to adjust our expectations and aim for sufficient closure. This may simply involve recognizing that we made an honest *attempt* to break through their self-deception. If we tie closure to actually succeeding in that effort, we'll keep reliving the memory unnecessarily. In our initial attempts, we should rely primarily on the role-reversal tests discussed earlier instead of revisiting the memory to come up with logical arguments.

We Expect to Have a Story With Just Outcomes

When something undesirable happens to us, we tend to construct a story around it. We often expect that story to reach closure through some form of justice. When we expect complete closure, it usually means we're hoping for the more conventional kind. The kind where the other person is held accountable and experiences consequences. As previously discussed, this involves just outcomes such as publicly holding the other person accountable and seeing them experience something undesirable that causes emotional suffering. When we cling to this idea of complete closure — and those conventional outcomes haven't been delivered — it can be difficult to stop reliving the memory.

In situations where obtaining conventional just outcomes is practically difficult, we can shift our expectations and aim for sufficient closure instead. This begins with recognizing that just outcomes still exist, but it's in the form of the emotional consequences the other person faces for acting against their own conscience. These internal consequences make it harder for them to reach their fundamental goal of happiness. We can also remind ourselves that the ultimate form of justice is our being happy, and that this happiness is as independent as possible from whether the other person suffers.

Even if we do get conventional justice, it may still not feel like complete closure if we were expecting it to make the wrong action feel as though it never happened. We may have hoped that this form of justice would "neatly square" with the wrongdoing and cancel it out.

No matter what form of justice we get — conventional or otherwise — it will never undo the action as if it never happened. It happened. If we keep seeking complete resolution in the form of justice that erases the event, we'll never stop revisiting the memory. Once again, we need to adjust our expectations and aim for sufficient resolution instead. To me, this means recognizing that, even though we can't undo what was done, we can still find peace, move on, and be happy.

We Expect to Find the Main Lessons of This Story

When we construct a story around an undesirable event, we also look to close it by identifying its main lessons. These become the key themes we associate with the story. The ideas that come to mind first when we recall it. They are what we say "this story is about". Without finding a theme that feels satisfying on some level, it's difficult to feel we've reached any closure.

We'll keep recalling the memory until we've identified these themes. But how many satisfying themes do we need to feel a sense of closure and stop the memory from resurfacing? While we may never uncover everything needed for complete closure, we can usually find enough to reach sufficient closure — and with that, we're able to move on.

For me, these are the key themes that typically provide sufficient closure when someone else has done the wrong thing.

The first theme is "how not to suffer". Through suffering, we came to learn the mental frameworks that caused us to respond that way to the action. We also learned how to dismantle them. While the memory may still remain, we no longer have to suffer because of it. We found a way to be at peace, move on, and be happy. This is a story about taking responsibility for our own suffering and our own happiness.

The second theme is "how to stop blaming ourselves". It's often easy to blame ourselves for "allowing" someone else's wrongdoing to happen. But we shouldn't hold ourselves responsible just because someone else failed to understand how to do the right thing. We aren't to blame for their actions or their ignorance. It makes even less sense to punish ourselves for what someone else chose to do. Learning to let go of this self-blame can be a deeply satisfying theme.

The third theme is "how to show others that they don't need to suffer". When we learn to dismantle the mental frameworks behind our suffering, we're also better equipped to help others break free from the same patterns. There is something satisfying in being able to help someone we care about so that they don't suffer in the ways that we have. For me, I like being able to demonstrate to others how to be happy despite what has happened. I like to show what is possible.

REASON #4: WE HAVE FRAMED THE IMMORAL ACTION AS "BIG" OR "INTERESTING"

When we frame someone's immoral behavior as "big" or "interesting", we signal to our mind that the action deserves attention. As a result, the memory is recalled more often.

In my view, this framing is conditioned into us by others and isn't inherent to the action itself. Another person could experience the same wrongdoing, but if they don't frame it as "big" or "interesting", they recall the memory far less. They're simply not signaling to their mind that the action deserves attention.

For this reason, I think we should make an effort, where possible, not to apply these kinds of framings to wrongful actions. When we stop using such labels, the actions feel far more mundane. And once the memory becomes boring to us, we stop paying attention to it and recall it far less. Our attention is instead freed up for far more interesting things happening in the present and future.

For the record, I consider it quite boring when someone decides to do the wrong thing. It's the easiest thing one can find in themselves to do. It's bizarre that people would elect to be so boring. What I find far more compelling is when someone finds the strength to do the right thing and act in line with their conscience. Doing the wrong thing requires no strength at all.

REASON #5: WE ARE TRYING TO IMPRESS THE PERSON WHO WRONGED US

When someone wrongs us, our ego may want to impress them by showing how well our life is going. As a result, it keeps replaying hypothetical encounters in which we talk about how great things are. This mental rehearsal can keep the memory alive. But when we convince our ego to stop trying to impress them, we tend to recall the memory less. Ironically, the *least impressive* thing is to let ourselves be controlled by our ego, such that we spend time imagining how to impress the other person.

The most impressive thing we can do is actually control our ego so we don't dwell on these hypothetical encounters. As a result, if we come across this person, we haven't prepared anything to make them think highly of us. We're perfectly comfortable walking away from that conversation with them feeling unimpressed. We don't even need to share how little we think about them. Instead of thinking about how to impress them, we use that time doing other things that are more satisfying.

It can also help us let go of trying to impress the other person when we consider that their range of possible reactions — whether impressed or not — is unlikely to be interesting or useful to us. There are far more worthwhile and engaging things we could be thinking about or doing instead.

REASON #6: WE ARE FIGHTING THE MEMORY EVERY TIME IT APPEARS

It may be that our ego is attached to having the power to *completely* erase this memory from our mind. It can't tolerate the memory even briefly surfacing. As a result, whenever it does appear, we find ourselves trying to "fight" it in order to make it go away.

However, by fighting it, we actually give it more *attention*, which serves to make it linger longer in our minds. The memory stays alive because our ego keeps it alive. If we can get the ego to stop clinging to the need for control and become more tolerant of its presence, it will no longer react when the thought appears. As a result, we stop feeding it attention. Without resistance, the memory doesn't remain for long — it simply passes through.

Our ego's attachment to this ability can also lead to feelings of powerlessness, helplessness, and anger each time it surfaces. This emotional distress isn't caused by the memory itself, but by the ego's fixation on this form of control. When we help the ego let go, the thought can arise without triggering that pain.

Our lack of tolerance for the memory may also stem from the belief that its presence makes happiness impossible. In other words, we've adopted a happiness conditional statement tied to its appearance. Because of this belief, we fight it when it surfaces, which again only makes it linger longer. To undo this belief and stop resisting, we need to recognize that happiness is still possible, even when the memory arises.

Our belief in this happiness condition can also lead to despair whenever the memory arises. This distress isn't caused by the past itself, but by the belief that happiness is impossible. Once we let go of that belief, the despair should fade as well.

To increase our tolerance for the memory, we should *accept* that it's part of our life and will likely resurface from time to time. The more we accept this, the more mundane it becomes, and the less attention we give it.

BE MINDFUL OF OTHER REASONS WE RECALL THE MEMORY

In this chapter, we looked at how to challenge five of the most common reasons for recalling a memory of an undesirable event. If, after addressing these five, we still find ourselves frequently thinking about a particular memory, it's likely because there are other unexamined reasons our mind is using to bring it up.

If the memory is still providing genuinely useful information, it may be worth continuing to recall it. But if it isn't, we should try to identify the other reasons our mind keeps bringing it up, so we can challenge them directly and stop reliving it.

That said, we may not need to gather all these reasons to stop reliving the memory. Instead, we can form the habit of thinking that, *regardless of the reason*, recalling this particular memory is unlikely to be interesting, useful, or satisfying. It doesn't matter what rationale the mind offers; we could be spending our time on things in the present that are far more worthwhile.

BECOMING MORE EFFICIENT AT "PROCESSING" THIS MEMORY

When an undesirable action occurs, our goal should be to find peace, move on, and return to happiness as quickly as possible. This means reducing both the intensity and duration of our emotional suffering in response to the event. It also means minimizing how often we revisit the memory. The sooner we "process" and let it go, the more time we can devote to things that are more interesting, useful, and enjoyable.

We become more efficient at this process by making it a habit to dismantle the mental frameworks that cause emotional suffering *as soon as* the undesirable action occurs. These often involve the ego or happiness conditional statements. By disassembling them quickly, we reduce our mental susceptibility to suffer in response to the action. We want to reach a point where, by habit, it becomes difficult for us to generate these mental patterns in the first place. At the same time, we should get into the habit of immediately questioning the mind's reasons for recalling the event, so we don't keep reliving it unnecessarily.

4

———

HOW WE BUILD OUR
MODEL OF REALITY

So far, we've examined how to dismantle mental frameworks that diminish our enjoyment and generate emotional pain. By breaking down these patterns of thought, we reduce their interference with the playful mind and our openness to the present moment.

Now, we'll turn to another potential source of interference: our drive to build a model of reality. This model reflects our understanding of what reality is and how it functions — specifically, *the cause-and-effect relationships within it.* That is, when one event occurs, another tends to follow. Each cause-and-effect relationship we identify serves as a "building block" in this model. The more of these relationships we understand, the more blocks we add, and the more complete our picture of reality becomes.

A strong urge to build this model can disrupt the playful mind. In pursuing this drive, we may become so focused on constructing a coherent picture of reality that we lose our openness to the present. The search for answers to the "big" questions can pull our attention away, causing us to overlook what's right in front of us.

To remove this interference, we don't need to 100% complete our model. This is fortunate, as it is impossible for us to understand everything there is about reality. We only need a version that feels complete enough to put us at ease, one that no longer preoccupies us to the point of missing out on the present.

In my view, for most people, "complete enough" involves grasping the "foundational building blocks" in sufficient detail. These foundational components support all other understanding built upon them. We'll explore these in the chapters that follow. In this chapter, we'll focus on understanding the steps involved in building this model, as doing so is part of satisfying this drive.

THE STEPS INVOLVED IN BUILDING A MODEL OF REALITY

As previously mentioned, our model of reality is our comprehension of what reality is and how it operates. It is our explanation of the cause-and-effect relationships within reality.

But what, more specifically, are we forming our understanding in response to? It's the experiences we observe. When we *see* something happen, we try to understand what caused it. In other words, we observe an experience and then attempt to grasp the cause-and-effect relationships within it. For example, suppose we enjoy birdwatching. Each time we do, we might focus on observing a particular bird. Based on what we see and hear in its natural habitat, we begin to form an understanding of its behavior and why it behaves that way.

This explanation of our observed experiences becomes a component we add to our overall picture of reality. To summarize: we build our model of reality from what we observe. It reflects our entire comprehension of the causal relationships we've encountered. And it goes far beyond bird behavior. It includes everything we've come to understand about economics, physics, philosophy, society, human nature, technology, and more. The more experiences we observe, the more explanations we tend to generate, and the more building blocks we add to our version of reality.

How We Adapt Our Model to Our Observations

When we observe a new experience, we not only try to grasp its causal relationships, we also check whether it conflicts with what we currently believe about reality. Does anything in our existing model suggest that what we've seen *shouldn't* have happened? For example, as we continue observing the bird, we assess whether its behavior aligns with our most recent view of it.

There are two possible outcomes of this check.

If our current model includes an explanation that suggests the experience shouldn't have happened, then that explanation has been *contradicted* by what we observed. We should replace any building blocks containing the outdated explanation with one that is logically consistent with the new observation. This "replacement explanation" must take this new experience into account when trying to explain reality. This process of removing and replacing explanations can be seen as us *adapting* our model of reality in response to what we observe.

Let's say our current model suggests that this particular bird only drinks fresh water and never drinks saltwater. We believe its body can't process saltwater, which is why it avoids it. But one day, we observe many birds of this species drinking from a saltwater source. Over several days, we see them return to this same body of water to drink. This observation contradicts our earlier understanding of the bird's behavior. In adapting our picture of reality, we now recognize not only that the bird drinks saltwater, but also that its body is capable of processing it.

Alternatively, if no explanation in our current model suggests that the experience shouldn't have happened, then our existing explanations are logically consistent with it. No components of our model need to be replaced. Instead, we simply incorporate our understanding of the new experience as an additional building block. In this case, rather than adapting our model of reality, we're building upon it.

Let's say we observe the bird using a vocal call to attract mates.

This particular call is one we haven't heard before. Our current picture of reality doesn't suggest that such a call couldn't exist, so the observation doesn't contradict what we've already gathered. We can simply add our understanding of this newly observed behavior to our existing view of the bird.

To summarize this mental process of refining the model: we are *assessing* or *testing* the logical consistency of our current understanding of reality against the new experience. We're looking for any building blocks that the observation may have contradicted.

A Summary of the Steps Involved in Building and Adapting Our Model

From the above, we can outline a basic view of the steps involved in constructing and refining our picture of reality:

Step #1: We *observe* an experience. For example, we see and hear the bird in its natural habitat.

Step #2: We *think* about the experience we have observed so we can *understand* it. In this thought, we formulate a view of the causal relationships within this experience. For instance, we reflect on what we've seen and heard of the bird's behavior and try to grasp why it behaves that way.

Step #3: We *think* about whether our current model suggests that the experience we've just observed shouldn't have happened. Has what we've just seen and heard about this bird contradicted what we currently understand about it?

There are two possible outcomes from this examination.

If our current model is *contradicted* by the observation, we replace the conflicting explanation with one that is logically consistent. We discard our previous understanding of the bird and update it to better reflect what we've witnessed. By doing so, we *adapt* our model of reality to fit the new experience.

If our current model is *consistent* with the observation, we simply incorporate our understanding of the new experience without removing or replacing anything. We retain our existing view of the bird's behavior and expand on it. This is us *building* on our existing model without altering what's already there.

Step #4: Repeat Steps #1, #2, and #3. As in, repeat the process of *observing* and *thinking* about what we've observed. We keep seeing, hearing, and thinking about the bird, which continuously increases our understanding of its behavior. This ongoing process allows us to *continually build* and *adapt* our model of reality.

It is particularly vital that we keep repeating Step #3 every time we observe a new experience. Without it, our picture of reality may not stay logically consistent with all our observations.

CAN WE EVER UNDERSTAND ANYTHING IN REALITY WITH *CERTAINTY*?

Let's distinguish between understanding something with certainty and understanding it with uncertainty.

To have *certainty* is to possess an understanding of causal relationships that is *impossible* to be contradicted by any experience. We have proven that reality must behave this way. It is not possible for it to behave otherwise. So, when we add this building block to our model of reality, we are adding an understanding that we absolutely *know* to be true.

To have *uncertainty* means holding an understanding of causal relationships that is *possible* to be contradicted by an experience. We have not proven that reality must behave this way. It is possible that it operates differently from our explanation here. So, when we add this building block to our picture of reality, we are adding an understanding that we only *believe* to be true, not what we know to be true. At best, we may believe this explanation is true with high confidence. But we still acknowledge there's a chance it isn't.

To sum it up: certainty means we're 100% sure reality matches our view; uncertainty means we're less than 100% sure.

So back to the question at hand: can we ever understand anything in reality with certainty? Can we ever understand something in a way that is genuinely beyond the possibility of contradiction?

In my view, the answer is no. We can never be certain about any part of our model of reality, nor can we prove that reality must behave as we conceive it. This outcome seems logically inevitable, as our model is limited to the experiences we've had, and there will always be things we have *not observed*. These "unobserved experiences" are that which we may:

- Observe at some point in the future but have not yet.
- Never observe due to never being in the right place at the right time.

There are also "unobservable experiences": things we simply can't sense because of our biological limits. For example, animals like dogs and bats can smell and hear things that we can't. Even if we were in the right place at the right time, we still wouldn't be able to experience them. We can describe many of them scientifically, but we have no way to perceive them directly, and no real sense of what they would feel like. Because they're beyond what we're capable of biologically experiencing, we can't even imagine them clearly. It's like trying to picture a color you've never seen or a smell you've never had. Since we have no frame of reference, we can't really imagine what they would be like.

Given the above, we cannot prove with 100% certainty that our explanation of reality is immune to contradiction by an unobserved or unobservable experience. Anything less than 100% certainty — including 99% — is not a certainty. Even our collective understanding of what we call "scientific laws" today could be *completely rewritten* if a new experience came along tomorrow which contradicted all of it. These "scientific laws" are better thought of as "scientific hypotheses" that, strictly speaking, are never proven but tested again and again with observation. While our current scientific understanding *appears* true based on observation, we have not proven it. The actual truth may differ from our explanations. This idea of viewing scientific laws as "perpetual hypotheses" is not new to the scientific community.

To be clear: it might very well be that our current explanation of our observations is logically consistent with all the things we haven't observed. The issue is that we have no way of proving this. Strictly speaking, we can't comment *either way* on whether our current understanding would be logically consistent with or contradicted by unobserved things. Any comments we make in either direction about our unobserved experiences would be completely uninformed. So, while our current conception of reality *may* align with the truth, we just can't prove or know that it does. At most, we can only *believe* it does. To put it another way: reality may behave exactly as we conceive it — we just can't prove it.

Why Repeated Observation Still Falls Short of Proof

It is useful to recognize how our scientific understanding — often regarded as proven with 100% certainty — could still be contradicted by an unobserved experience. We generally regard scientific understanding as beyond reproach because it appears to be reinforced by *repeated observation*. As in, we have repeatedly observed this specific "Cause A" leading to this specific "Effect B". From these repeated observations, it would be reasonable to believe that there is a causal relationship between A and B. This belief might very well align with what is true. Reality might indeed behave in accordance with this explanation.

However, we cannot rule out the possibility that some unobserved factor is repeatedly causing Effect B. It could very well be the case that A is not exerting any causal influence on B at all. This other mysterious factor could be some particle we have not yet detected or cannot detect. Or it could be some entity we cannot perceive. It could be something we can't even imagine. Given this, even repeated observation can't rule out the potential that reality operates differently than we think.

Now, I'm not suggesting we reject our entire scientific understanding or other views we've formed through repeated observation. Using repeated observation to generate explanations is the best tool we have, but it is a tool with limits. Its greatest limit is that it cannot prove, with 100% certainty, that we've arrived at the truth. At most, we can use this tool of repeated observation to generate understandings that we believe with high confidence are consistent with our experiences. But we must always accept the possibility that this view could be contradicted by what remains unobserved. So, while I believe current science to be true with high confidence, I also accept the chance that it may not be. I believe reality behaves this way, while always leaving room for the potential that it might not.

Why Shared Belief Is Not the Same as Proof

But what about understandings formed through the repeated observations of not just one individual, but multiple? When other people have arrived at the same explanation through repeated observation, is that now proven with 100% certainty? No, it isn't. All these people have is a *shared belief* in the same understanding. They haven't eliminated the possibility of this view being contradicted by some other factor *beyond their collective observations*. This factor might be something humans are biologically capable of observing, but simply haven't yet. Or it could be something we are biologically incapable of observing and therefore will never experience. It could even be something that is beyond our collective imagination to consider. When it comes down to it, reality could still operate differently from this shared belief.

So even if every single human on the planet shares the same view, it still hasn't been proven with 100% certainty. Even together, we can't eliminate the possibility that it could be contradicted by something none of us have observed. All we have here still is a *shared belief* in the same explanation. There is also no requirement that we human beings can truly understand the universe. Just as there's no requirement that a dog can comprehend how the universe works, there's no guarantee that we can either. While we hope to arrive at the truth, it is not something that is owed to us by virtue of being human. Any sense of entitlement is just our ego talking. In my view, we're lucky if the explanations we form in response to our experiences happen to be true.

A MODEL OF REALITY BUILT ENTIRELY ON BELIEF

If we can never understand anything with certainty, how does that impact the model of reality we can build?

The impact is that our *entire model of reality* — that is, our entire understanding of the causal relationships within our observed experiences — is made of what we *believe* to be true. Every building block contains an understanding that we can only believe *appears logically consistent* and not what we know to be logically consistent. There is no part of the model that we know or have proven to be true. To be clear: it's possible that parts of our picture are true. It's even possible that all of it is. We just can't confirm it.

From this, we can establish a baseline definition of a model of reality: it is the sum of our explanations for the causal relationships within the experiences we've observed so far. The phrase "experiences we've observed so far" is key. It highlights that our entire understanding, at any given moment, is *limited* to what we've observed up to that point. Since our model of reality is made entirely of belief, we must always allow for the possibility that everything we've understood so far could be contradicted by something unobserved. We must always accept that any part of our current picture might need to be revised in light of a future experience. This is why any model of reality we put forward shouldn't be seen as a declaration of how reality operates, but rather as a *working suggestion*. It is simply a set of beliefs based on what we've observed until now.

We must also always accept the possibility that an experience *we never observe* could contradict our current understanding. However, that doesn't mean our understanding will change because of it. Since we never encounter the experience, we can't identify which parts of our model it contradicts. And if we can't detect the flawed components, we can't replace them. We can only adapt our model of reality in response to experiences we've actually observed, not to those we haven't.

Is It Worth Searching for Contradictions from Unobserved Things?

Should we actively seek out things we haven't observed that might contradict our current conception of reality? There isn't any point in trying to find experiences we're biologically incapable of observing. But what about those we may observe in the future? Should we try to encounter them sooner? And what about experiences we might never come across simply because we're not in the right place at the right time? Should we attempt to put ourselves there somehow?

I can appreciate why someone might see this as the prudent thing to do. The sooner we encounter experiences that contradict our current model, the sooner we can identify which building blocks are flawed and replace them with ones that are logically consistent. The thinking in this approach is to make our picture of reality more logically consistent with unobserved things.

Generally, I would say that we shouldn't actively try to find such experiences. This is for two reasons.

First, we're only talking about a *potential* contradiction in our current model, one that could arise from an experience we haven't observed. But that experience may not even exist, and if it doesn't, the contradiction won't either. Reality might actually behave just as we currently think it does. If we go looking for such experiences, we risk spending a great deal of time searching for something that isn't there.

Second, we should focus on finding parts of our model that are contradicted by things we've already observed, rather than things we haven't. Instead of trying to resolve hypothetical contradictions based on unobserved experiences, we should focus on correcting the errors revealed by what we've actually seen. This includes not just recent experiences, but also those we may have encountered long ago, even in childhood.

The more we focus on correcting these errors, the more logically consistent our view of reality becomes with what we've already observed. Resolving existing discrepancies tends to bring faster benefits. When we better understand how to attain our wants or which harmful thought patterns to discard, it leads to greater enjoyment and less distress. By contrast, trying to resolve potential contradictions may offer no such benefits if no actual contradiction exists.

Why We Don't Always Spot Contradictions Right Away

How is it that we can have so many building blocks in our model that were contradicted by experiences we encountered long ago? And why haven't we removed them after all this time? This might seem puzzling. After all, when we first observed the contradicting experience, we looked for parts of our current understanding it might challenge. So the contradictory component should have been identified at the time and replaced.

The problem is that during the initial search, we usually examine only *parts of our model* — not the entire picture. If we happen to check the building blocks that are contradicted by the experience, we can replace them. But if we focus only on components that align with the experience, we may not notice that it actually contradicts another part of our understanding. We won't see any need for an update, so the flawed building blocks remain and continue to shape how we think reality works.

Let's return to the birdwatching example, but now we're observing a different species. One day, we see this bird trying to reach prey trapped behind bark on a log. After several failed attempts at pecking the bark, it flies off and returns with a small stick in its beak. It uses the stick to peel away the bark and then impale the insect. The bird pulls the stick back with the insect on it and eats it. At first, we think this observation aligns with our current understanding of the bird's hunting habits, and we don't see anything that appears to contradict what we believe.

What we don't realize is that seeing the bird use a stick as a hunting tool suggests a higher level of intelligence than our current thinking allows. We've previously formed a firm view, based on past observations, that this bird isn't particularly smart. We miss the inconsistency because we haven't yet compared what we just saw with what we currently believe about the bird's intelligence.

I'm not suggesting that, upon first encountering a new experience, we should search through our entire model of reality to compare it with that observation. Doing so would take a very long time and be highly inefficient, especially if we tried it with every new experience. Instead, it's better to hold off on forming a firm view of the new observation until we've checked a larger portion of our model for contradictions.

In any case, we do *eventually* identify many of the contradictory components we've accidentally added to our picture of reality. That's because, throughout our lives, we *continue searching* — consciously or subconsciously — for building blocks that conflict with experiences we've already observed. Even if we're not deliberately engaging in this search, I believe we can't help but do it on some level. While we may not notice every discrepancy right away, we often end up spotting them later.

Do We Ultimately Need to Resolve Every Contradiction We've Accumulated?

In my view, no. We just need our understanding of reality to be consistent *enough* to help us attain what we want. Until we do, there may be a strong incentive to resolve flaws in our thinking. But once we've *attained* those wants, the motivation to correct any remaining errors in our model tends to diminish.

Let's say, hypothetically, we manage to resolve enough of the contradictions created by our observed experiences, perhaps even all of them. With all of that out of the way, should we go looking for contradictions in experiences we haven't had yet but could?

I think this comes down to personal preference as to how one wants to spend their time. It can be useful, and even fun, to seek out new experiences that might contradict our current view of things. On some level, it can be enjoyable to "stress test" the logical consistency of our beliefs. But again, we might be chasing a contradiction that doesn't exist. Personally, I'd rather spend that time enjoying the present. Of course, we can switch between the two. We don't have to commit to just one. That said, we should actively seek new experiences when we've identified errors in our thinking that we can't resolve with our current information. In those cases, new data and new observations are necessary to fix the errors.

Key Takeaways About Our Model of Reality

I appreciate that the previous section may be a lot to take in. To make things clearer, here are the main takeaways:

- Our "model of reality" is best described as *our entire understanding of the causal relationships within the experiences we have observed so far.*
- Because this model is built entirely on belief — not certainty — we must always leave room for the possibility that our understanding could change in the future based on new experiences. There's a chance that reality behaves differently from everything we currently think.
- Our goal should be to make our picture of reality logically consistent *enough* with our observed experiences to help us attain what we want.

We may resist accepting the total absence of certainty, believing that happiness is impossible without it. In other words, we've adopted a happiness conditional statement; one that tricks us into thinking we need certainty in order to be happy. But in my view, we don't need to prove our explanations are true to experience this satisfying mental state. We just need to arrive at something we honestly believe is logically consistent with what we've observed so far. Once we discard this happiness condition, it becomes easier to accept that we can never grasp anything with certainty.

Any despair we feel from not being able to prove we have the truth also stems from this happiness condition. Without that belief, the despair wouldn't exist.

WHAT *DISRUPTS* OUR ABILITY TO ADAPT OUR MODEL OF REALITY TO NEW EXPERIENCES

As previously mentioned, when we replace the contradictory parts of our model after encountering a new experience, we have "adapted" our model to that experience. This process of updating our model to fit new observations is a vital one. It helps us keep it logically consistent with all the experiences we have seen to date.

However, there are times when we observe a new experience that contradicts our picture of reality, *yet we don't remove the conflicting building blocks.* In these cases, we haven't adapted our model to the new observation. Without an update, the model continues to carry components that are now contradicted by what we've just seen. As a result, our understanding of how reality operates falls out of sync with our observations.

There are two scenarios in which this adaptation does not occur.

Scenario #1 is one we've already seen. When we observe something new, we start looking for contradictions, but only examine the parts of our model that align with the new observation. As a result, we may not realize that other parts are actually being contradicted. At this stage, we're unaware of any conflict in our thinking. It's only later, perhaps after further reflection or new experiences, that we recognize the error and revise our model.

To revisit the birdwatching example from the previous section: we see a bird using a stick as a hunting tool and ask whether this behavior fits our view of its hunting habits. What we don't realize is that this observation actually contradicts our belief that the bird has low intelligence. This happens because we haven't evaluated the new behavior against our assumptions about the bird's cognitive ability.

Scenario #2 is one we haven't discussed yet. It begins the same way; we encounter a new experience and start looking for contradictions in our thinking. This time, we actually find them. However, despite *honestly believing deep down* that these conflicting components exist in our model, we still don't remove them. We still don't fix the contradiction.

Returning to the birdwatching example, we may already recognize, beneath the surface, that our belief in the bird's low intelligence has been contradicted by what we've seen. Yet we continue to keep this belief as part of our picture of reality.

What's Happened in Scenario #2?

When a new experience leads us to genuinely believe that part of our model no longer reflects how reality behaves, we typically respond in one of two ways: we either *consciously accept* the contradiction or *consciously deny* it.

To "consciously accept" the contradiction means allowing what we honestly believe deep down about reality to *emerge consciously*. In other words, it means being honest with ourselves that reality does not behave as we previously understood it. Once we've consciously acknowledged an error in our model, we can begin replacing the contradictory parts with something more logically consistent. Only through this kind of self-honesty can we actually adapt our picture of reality to the new experience we've observed.

In the birdwatching example, this would mean consciously acknowledging that our belief in the bird's low intelligence is no longer valid. We can then replace it with a more refined view of the bird's advanced cognitive ability.

To "consciously deny" the contradiction means *not* allowing what we honestly believe deep down about reality to reach conscious awareness. Instead of being honest with ourselves, we deceive the conscious mind into believing there is no contradiction and that reality still behaves according to our current understanding. In doing so, we become caught in self-deception.

But this deception affects only the conscious mind. On a deeper level, the subconscious still recognizes that a contradiction exists, that reality no longer aligns with our current model. As a result of this denial, the conflicting building block remains in our picture instead of being removed. And for as long as we continue to deceive ourselves in this way, we prevent our model of reality from adapting to the experience we've just observed.

In the birdwatching example, to consciously deny the discrepancy is to reject the idea that our belief in the bird's low intelligence has been challenged. We convince ourselves that this belief still logically aligns with what we've seen. Yet on a subconscious level, we continue to recognize the inconsistency. We still sense that the bird's behavior reveals a higher cognitive ability than we consciously think. And because we've deceived ourselves, we're unable to replace this incorrect belief with one that actually reflects the reality we observed.

Both Scenario #1 and Scenario #2 can result in us not adapting our version of reality to a new experience. But there's an important distinction between them.

In Scenario #1, we don't adapt the model because we're completely unaware that the new experience contradicts it. We genuinely haven't realized that reality behaves differently from how we currently understand it. It's an innocent mistake.

In Scenario #2, we don't adapt the model because we're deceiving our conscious mind into thinking there is no contradiction. On some level — subconsciously — we are aware that the new experience doesn't align with our model. We sense that reality behaves differently from what we believe, but we consciously deny it. This is not an innocent error; it's self-deception.

Given how vital it is to adapt our picture of reality to new experiences, we should *protect* this ability. When we don't refine our model — whether due to an innocent error (Scenario #1) or self-deception (Scenario #2) — we undermine that adaptability. In these cases, we've allowed, unwittingly or not, building blocks that have been contradicted by observation to remain in our version of reality. To protect this adaptive ability, we need to reduce how often we let innocent errors and self-deceptions occur.

If we want to reduce the number of innocent errors we make on a particular topic, we should become more familiar with its fundamental principles. With these in mind, it becomes easier to spot what makes sense and what doesn't. Other than that, we can aim to generally be "more careful", and take more time when forming our thoughts.

If we want to minimize how often we deceive ourselves, we need to investigate why we have this tendency in the first place.

Why Is It So Hard to Consciously Admit When There's a Contradiction in Our Thinking?

One reason is this: we leverage our understanding to exert control over our reality and attain what we want. Being in control and reaching desired outcomes is often why we seek to understand things in the first place. When we have an explanation of something that we believe is logically consistent, this gives us a *greater feeling of control* over our reality. But when we encounter a contradiction, we *feel a loss of that control.* We can call them "feelings of destabilization".

These feelings of destabilization can be uncomfortable and unpleasant to experience consciously, and we generally prefer to avoid them. This is why, when we encounter an experience that contradicts our thinking, there's a tendency to consciously deny the inconsistency. We want to avoid the emotional discomfort that comes with recognizing flaws in our explanations. By denying the existence of the error, the conscious mind shields itself from these uncomfortable feelings. That said, conscious denial does not mean these destabilizing feelings are completely eliminated from our mind. They stay suppressed in the subconscious, which remains aware of the error in our model.

Even though we may feel the urge to deny a contradiction in order to avoid uncomfortable emotions, we don't always act on that impulse. When we encounter an experience that makes us believe deep down there's a contradiction, we may still consciously accept it, despite the emotional discomfort. After we acknowledge it, there's a period of adjustment as we get used to the idea that the discrepancy exists and that reality behaves differently than we thought. From this place of conscious acceptance, the destabilizing feelings dissipate.

What allows us to acknowledge a contradiction, even when we want to avoid the destabilizing emotions that come with it? The answer is mental fortitude. "Mental fortitude" refers to the mental and emotional strength to consciously *withstand* uncomfortable or unpleasant feelings. When we accept flaws in our picture of reality, it's because we have enough fortitude to tolerate the emotional discomfort they bring. As mentioned, while these feelings may enter conscious awareness, they fade after a period of adjustment — we don't have to carry them forever. When we lack sufficient mental fortitude, however, we tend to deny the flaw exists in order to avoid the discomfort.

It may come as a surprise that our ability to adapt our model of reality isn't determined by how "logical" or "smart" we are. Instead, it depends on whether we have the *mental and emotional strength* to bear the turbulence that arises when we discover errors in our thinking. Only with this kind of mental fortitude can we keep our picture of reality consistent with what we've actually observed.

How to Increase Our Capacity to Admit When We're Wrong

Given how important our mental and emotional strength is to understanding reality, it makes sense to invest in developing it. As we strengthen this capacity, we increase the amount of emotional discomfort we're able — and willing — to consciously tolerate. The more we can handle these destabilizing feelings, the less likely we are to deny the existence of an error. As your mental fortitude grows, you'll find it much harder to fall into self-deception — and much easier to break free from the ones already in place.

We can strengthen our mental fortitude by focusing on the benefits of adapting our model of reality to match our observed experiences. Specifically, we can reflect on how this adaptation affects what matters most to us: our satisfaction and suffering. The more logically consistent our model is with our observations, the better it can guide us toward greater fulfillment and less pain. But when we neglect to refine it, our understanding becomes riddled with contradictions and less effective at guiding us toward happiness.

We can also lessen the intensity of the destabilizing feelings that arise when we encounter contradictions in our model. The weaker these feelings are, the easier they are for the conscious mind to tolerate, and the less mental fortitude is needed to endure them. When we come across an experience that challenges our explanations, the intensity of our emotional response depends on *how much of our model* we think is being contradicted. The more aspects we see as undermined, the greater the sense of losing control over our reality, which in turn heightens the destabilizing feelings.

Often, when we encounter an experience that challenges our views, we panic and overestimate how much of our model is actually being contradicted. This overreaction leads us to generate far more destabilizing emotions than the situation warrants. At times like these, it's important to recognize that the experience likely contradicts *a small part of the model and not more than that*. In most cases, the rest of the model should still be logically consistent. So, while we may have less control now in one aspect of our reality, we still retain it in others.

It also helps to reduce these destabilizing emotions by recognizing that discovering discrepancies in our model often puts us in the best position to gain the control we thought we had. By identifying the contradiction, we can replace the flawed thinking with something more accurate. This act of refining our understanding increases our level of control over reality.

It can be difficult to accept that we're deceiving ourselves, especially if it brings feelings of embarrassment or shame. But I don't think anyone should feel that way. Every one of us is self-deceiving on some level about something. I don't believe we can eliminate all self-deception, but we can take steps to reduce it significantly, so it doesn't get in the way of attaining what we want.

HOW CAN WE TELL WHEN OUR CONSCIOUS MIND IS DECEIVING ITSELF AND WHEN IT IS BEING HONEST?

The challenge of being caught in a self-deception is that it can be very difficult to tell that we are in one. While we may be subconsciously aware that a contradiction exists in our views, we consciously believe that this part of our model is logically consistent. Our conscious mind thinks it's being honest with itself.

Even when there's no self-deception and our conscious mind is genuinely being honest in thinking this part of the model is logically consistent, doubt can't be fully extinguished. We still can't rule out the possibility that we're deceiving ourselves. We may *believe* our conscious mind is being sincere, but we can't know it with certainty or prove that it is.

That said, there is a way to gain confidence that our conscious mind is being honest with itself about specific parts of the model: by observing whether we exhibit behavioral patterns consistent with genuine self-honesty. While these patterns don't provide definitive proof, they offer strong evidence that we're being honest with ourselves. On the other hand, if we notice ourselves displaying the opposite behaviors, it's a strong indication that self-deception is at play. A person whose conscious mind is sincerely being honest has no reason to behave in that way.

Three behavioral patterns are especially suggestive of self-honesty on a given topic.

First, a person who is honest with themselves can always acknowledge the possibility that their belief might be incorrect. After all, no one on Earth can know or prove their beliefs are true with 100% certainty. Such a person may still be highly confident in their view, but they remain open to the chance that they're wrong. By contrast, someone who refuses to admit this possibility — despite being unable to rule it out — is likely deceiving themselves.

Second, a person who is sincere with themselves can always acknowledge the possibility that they might be engaged in self-deceit. They may still feel highly confident in their beliefs and in their own honesty, yet remain open to the chance that they're lying to themselves. By contrast, someone who refuses to admit this possibility — again, despite having no way to rule it out — is likely caught in it.

As mentioned earlier, accepting our capacity for self-deception can be difficult because of shame or embarrassment. But once we recognize there's no reason to feel that way, it becomes easier to acknowledge this capacity.

Third, a person who is honest with themselves is generally more willing and open to having conversations with people they disagree with. This is because they sincerely believe their understanding is logically consistent with the experiences they've had so far. They tend to be more confident in these discussions while still accepting the possibility that they could be wrong.

By contrast, a person who is already deceiving themselves on a particular topic tends to be less willing and less open to engaging with those who hold a different view. This is often because, on a subconscious level, they're aware that a contradiction exists in their thinking. Lacking the mental fortitude to tolerate the emotional discomfort that comes with recognizing this error, they avoid challenging conversations and instead surround themselves with people who won't challenge them.

Can Agreement from Others Prove We're Not Fooling Ourselves?

If many people agree with our view, does that prove our explanation is true with 100% certainty? And does that prove, by extension, that our conscious mind isn't deceiving itself on this topic? As discussed earlier, widespread agreement on an idea is not proof that it's true. Even if many people agree with us, all it shows is that we collectively share the same belief. None of us can rule out the possibility that an experience — outside of what we've collectively observed — might contradict that belief. It could be something we haven't yet observed, or something we never will. Because we can't eliminate this possibility, we cannot prove whether the shared belief aligns with what is actually true.

Even if widespread agreement doesn't prove our view is true, does it somehow still prove that we're all being honest with ourselves about the subject? That, given the limited data we have on reality, we've reached conclusions we can't prove, but at least we sincerely believe in it? After all, how could so many people be fooling themselves? Surely, we can't all be caught in the same self-deception.

Unfortunately, we can't rule out that scenario with 100% certainty. It's entirely possible for many people to be subconsciously aware of the *same contradiction* in their model of reality. If they all lack the mental fortitude to consciously tolerate the uncomfortable emotions that come with recognizing that contradiction, they may each avoid it in the same way. In doing so, their conscious minds all enter the same self-deception that this part of the model is logically consistent. Deep down, however, they're all aware it isn't.

As mentioned above, a person caught in self-deception often seeks out like-minded individuals who are unlikely to mention the discrepancy. They hope that widespread agreement serves as proof that their view is correct. They may resist acknowledging that such agreement doesn't prove anything, and avoid considering the possibility that they are all caught in a shared self-deception.

If you're nervous that a belief you share with a group might be a form of self-deception, there are a few simple questions you can ask yourself to test this:

- Can all of you acknowledge the possibility that these views might be incorrect?
- Can all of you admit the possibility that you might be caught in a shared self-deception?
- How willing and open are all of you to engage with people who disagree with your views?

We Should Surround Ourselves With People Who Have High Mental Fortitude

Reading the above, one might conclude that the best way to break free from self-deception is to spend more time around people who disagree with us. After all, such individuals are more likely to point out contradictions in our model during conversation.

I do think we should make an effort to engage with more people like this. But we should also keep in mind that, even if they aren't caught in the same self-deception we are, they may still be deceiving themselves in other ways. Their own self-deceit can distort the information they share, making it an inaccurate reflection of what they sincerely believe deep down. This is why, generally speaking, our primary criteria for choosing who to converse with shouldn't be whether they agree or disagree with us. That's still an important factor, but not the most important one.

In my view, the key criterion is whether the person has strong mental fortitude; specifically, the kind that allows their conscious mind to remain honest with itself while facing emotionally destabilizing experiences. With this resilience, they're better able to acknowledge errors in their picture of reality and work through them. As a result, their model is more closely aligned with what they've actually observed. It's also more likely to reflect what they genuinely believe is logically consistent. They'll also be better equipped to spot errors or self-deception in our model, having already confronted those issues in their own.

If we want to find people with high mental fortitude, we can look for those who consistently demonstrate the three self-honest behaviors mentioned earlier. Someone with strong mental fortitude regularly refines their picture of reality and is more accustomed to the idea that their current beliefs might be mistaken or shaped by self-deception. They also recognize the value of engaging with those who hold opposing views.

It's also worth noting that even people with high mental fortitude may still deceive themselves in *some* aspects of their model. While they might have enough resilience to accept flaws in most parts of their worldview, there may be specific areas where the emotional discomfort is simply too great to bear. When they talk to us about these topics, the information they share might be distorted or shaped by self-deception. What they say may not fully reflect what they genuinely believe deep down. It's rare to find someone with enough mental fortitude to be fully honest with themselves across every subject area. The best we can do is seek out people who demonstrate high mental fortitude across *most topics*. Look for those who show self-honest behaviors in much of their thinking.

If we want to foster greater mental fortitude in those around us, we should openly talk about how self-deception can compromise our thinking — often without us realizing it. It also helps to discuss the direct connection between higher mental fortitude and keeping our model of reality adaptable to new experiences, which in turn leads to greater enjoyment and less pain.

WHY DO WE HONESTLY BELIEVE IN SOME EXPLANATIONS OVER OTHERS?

Earlier in this chapter, we looked at the general process by which individuals build their picture of reality: they observe an experience and then formulate an explanation of the causal relationships within it. This "explanation" represents their understanding of what they've observed.

Given that we cannot prove our particular explanation for an observed experience is true with 100% certainty, what makes us honestly believe in it? Since no explanation can be definitively proven, any explanation is theoretically possible. For every experience we observe, there are — at least in theory — an infinite number of possible explanations. Yet for each experience, we end up honestly believing in one particular explanation. Or, at the very least, we believe that one explanation is more probable than the others.

Do we *choose* the explanation we honestly believe in? No, we don't. We can't simply choose to believe we're astronauts if we haven't observed ourselves doing things we associate with being one. We either honestly believe an explanation, or we don't. We don't get to choose. Something *compels* us to believe one explanation over another. But what is that something?

In my view, it has to do with the physical structure of our brain. The brain's physical structure makes us *biologically predisposed* to believe a particular explanation for an observed experience while accounting for every piece of information and every past event we've encountered.

In an alternate reality, we might have been biologically predisposed to believe a *different explanation* for the same observation if either of the following were the case:

- Our brain had a different physical structure, but we had the same information and experiences.
- Our brain had the same physical structure, but we had different information and experiences.

In the future, our brain will undergo physical changes, and we will also accumulate new information and experiences. These changes could make us biologically predisposed to either maintain our current belief about a particular observation or to revise it. But once again, any shift in belief is not a matter of choice. It is something we are compelled into.

Given the above, I characterize everything I honestly believe as a manifestation of a "biological predisposition" or a "biological compulsion", not as a "choice".

5

THE FOUNDATIONAL BELIEFS
IN OUR MODEL OF REALITY

Now that we've examined how we build and adapt our view of reality to fit our observed experiences, the next step is to explore its foundational building blocks. As a reminder, understanding these helps us develop a model of reality that feels complete enough to free our attention for the present.

These are the foundational components covered in this book:

- What makes us believe we exist (This chapter)
- The present moment (This chapter)
- The self (This chapter)
- Our sense of right and wrong (See Chapter 6)
- A definition of life (See Chapter 7)
- How to improve the way we feel about life (See Chapter 8)
- The compulsion to continue living (See Chapter 9)
- Traits that are vital to satisfying relationships (See Chapter 10)

As you read Chapters 5–10, you'll find that the earlier foundational building blocks generally inform the later ones. Understanding them first will make the rest of the material much clearer.

WHAT MAKES US BELIEVE WE EXIST?

The building block of "what makes us believe we exist" is the most *foundational* of them all. Every other component in our model is built on top of it. It is the starting point for all other beliefs. It is the most fundamental belief we have. For me, that core belief is: "I believe I exist because I observe experiences and can build a model of reality from them".

For us to believe we exist, we rely on our ability to observe *experiences*. But what are the *fundamental types of experience* that lead us to form this belief? We can expand on the core belief expressed above by exploring these foundational types of experience more closely.

We can categorize our observed experiences into three fundamental types:

- Sensorial experience: These are *sensations* we observe through our sensory organs such as the eyes, ears, nose, tongue, and skin. These sensations can typically be described in terms of "sensorial satisfaction" and "sensorial suffering".
- Emotional experience: These are *feelings* that we have. They can typically be described in terms of "emotional satisfaction" and "emotional suffering". Happiness is just one type of emotional satisfaction among many.
- Conceptual experience: These are the *thoughts* we have. It is within these thoughts that we construct our model of reality.

Our reality is always articulated in terms of the fundamental types of experience — *sensations, feelings, and thoughts*. When we understand reality better, we're really gaining a clearer grasp of the cause-and-effect relationships within the sensorial, emotional, and conceptual experiences that make up our reality.

Now that we've identified these fundamental types of experience, we can rearticulate our most foundational belief with greater specificity. We can now clarify which types of experience lead us to believe we exist. This core belief might be phrased as: "I believe I exist because I observe sensorial, emotional, and conceptual experiences; and can build a model of reality from them".

Why Are We Drawn to Explain What We Experience?

We do this because we're trying to *optimize our experience*. That is, to increase satisfaction and reduce suffering. By learning these causal relationships, we gain insight into what produces both sensorial and emotional gratification. This allows us to create more fulfilling experiences. It also helps us recognize what causes sensorial and emotional pain, so we can reduce it. The more clearly we see these patterns in reality, the more conscious control we have over our levels of enjoyment and distress. Another way to put this is that we're trying to optimize our "well-being" — which can be understood in terms of sensations and feelings, both pleasant and unpleasant.

We already have a solid grasp of the causal relationships that drive our *sensorial* satisfaction and suffering. We eat specific foods because we enjoy their taste. We put on a sweater to stop feeling cold. With this understanding, we can generally keep ourselves reasonably comfortable on a sensorial level. As a result, there isn't an intense drive to explore these particular causal relationships much further.

By contrast, we don't have a strong understanding of the causal relationships that drive our *emotional* satisfaction and suffering. This is why we often find ourselves with too little of the former and far too much of the latter. As mentioned earlier in the book, many people tend to assume their contentment depends on attaining external outcomes. They believe their distress comes from not having these yet. However, once they attain them, the distress isn't alleviated, nor do they gain much lasting contentment from the achievement.

As per the premise of this book, our emotional enjoyment and pain are driven primarily by our *internal* thoughts. To optimize our emotional satisfaction, we have to do the following:

- Disassemble the mental frameworks that limit our enjoyment. The most common examples were discussed in Chapter 1.
- Disassemble the mental frameworks that cause us pain. These were covered in Chapter 2.
- Develop a sufficiently detailed model of reality. This is the focus of Chapters 4-10.

Once we complete this exercise, generating the playful mind becomes much easier. With this mindset, we're more open to engaging with each moment as it arises. This optimizes our emotional enjoyment by helping us draw happiness and other satisfying emotions from whatever we're engaged in. Without the playful mind, we interact less fully with the present and miss out on much of this happiness and fulfillment. While we may still experience some pleasant emotions, we don't generate nearly as many. For these reasons, I consider the playful mind the *optimal mental interface* to bring into each moment of reality.

The Function of Thought

When we recognize why we seek to understand our experiences — that is, why we think at all — it becomes clear that the function of thought is to optimize our satisfaction. We use thought to increase both sensorial and emotional gratification while reducing sensorial and emotional pain.

There is a common assumption that thinking is important and useful in itself. That we think for its own sake rather than to serve a larger purpose. In my view, thinking is only valuable to the extent that it creates satisfaction or alleviates suffering. Even idle thoughts about topics we find interesting can be a source of emotional enjoyment. And so, simply *having* such thoughts can optimize our overall well-being. For example, I find the filmmaking process fascinating, even though I have no intention of making films myself. But because the topic engages me, simply thinking about it can be emotionally satisfying. As for why we're drawn to thoughts that cause distress: we're often trying to resolve them, to understand how to escape the pain they generate. In this sense, focusing on such thoughts can be a step toward optimizing future satisfaction.

For a particular thought to fulfill its function, it only needs to be *correct enough* to produce the satisfaction we seek. It doesn't have to be 100% correct. Strictly speaking, we don't need to identify every contradiction in our thinking to reach the gratification we're after. The thought doesn't need to be perfectly logically consistent, just consistent enough to work.

The best way for a thought to fulfill its function is for it to be as simple as possible without being needlessly complex. When we rearticulate a thought in simpler terms, we can still experience the same enjoyment, but now with fewer words. What once required a thousand words might now take just ten. The thought becomes more *efficient* at delivering satisfaction without losing its effectiveness.

If the function of thought is to optimize our satisfaction and our model of reality is entirely made of thought, it follows that the model itself must share that same objective. This means our picture of reality only needs to be logically consistent enough, not perfectly or absolutely so. It also implies that the best model is the simplest one, not one weighed down by unnecessary complexity. Instead of relying on hundreds of books, we might rely on just five. By simplifying our model in this way, we fill it with explanations that are more efficient at helping us attain the enjoyment we seek.

WHAT IS THE PRESENT MOMENT?

We often talk about the "present moment" and wanting to be more engaged with it. However, we're not very clear with ourselves on what it actually is. It's a lot easier to engage with something we understand.

While we are alive, we are always in a single moment. Specifically, a single second. We mark the passage of time as movement from one moment to the next. We distinguish between present, past, and future moments based on their relationship to the moment we are currently experiencing. That which we call the "present moment".

We can understand the fundamental nature of a moment — whether present, past, or future — when we articulate it in terms of *experience*. As in, we can articulate a moment as the "combination of sensorial, emotional, and conceptual experiences we are observing at a given point in time". It is every sensation, feeling, and thought we are having at that exact instant.

Now that we've recognized a moment as the collection of our experiences within a single point in time, we can examine the fundamental characteristics of the present moment.

Firstly — and perhaps most importantly — the present moment is simply the combination of sensorial, emotional, and conceptual experiences we are observing at *this* point in time. So when we talk about "engaging with the present moment", we are, more specifically, engaging with this immediate blend of experiences.

Secondly, when we move from one moment to the next, what is happening is that the combination of sensorial, emotional, and conceptual experiences is *changing* within this moment. No present moment we enter is ever exactly the same as the ones that came before or the ones that follow. No person ever experiences the same moment twice in their lifetime. While some points in time may feel similar, they are never identical. The specific mix of sensations, feelings, and thoughts that make up a given moment never repeats itself exactly. There is always some variation. This makes each moment *utterly unique* compared to any other we experience.

Thirdly, the present is the *only* moment that ever exists at any point in time. Past and future moments do not exist right now. Past moments may have occurred before this point in time, but they are not happening right now. When we think about the past, we are just recalling memories of previous events that have survived into the present moment. These past moments exist only as memories. Like-wise, future moments may happen after this point in time, but they are also not happening right now. When we think about the future, we are extrapolating hypothetical events based on what is happening in the present moment and our memories of past moments. These future scenarios exist only as hypotheticals at this present point in time.

Fourthly, we experience the present moment only from our own perspective, not anyone else's. In each moment, we directly observe only our own sensorial, emotional, and conceptual experiences. Because we are not inside anyone else's mind, we cannot directly access their thoughts, sensations, or feelings. Instead, we infer the contents of their mind based on what they say and do. While we can't directly observe another person's internal experience, we can form beliefs about it through these external cues.

Where Is the Present Moment Being Physically Generated?

I'm not a neuroscientist, but I don't think it's a stretch to say that the present moment is physically generated by the brain. Likely in the form of electrical signals produced by some biochemical process. At any given instant, these signals contain all the sensorial, emotional, and conceptual experiences we're observing. I bring this up because understanding what the present moment *is* also requires understanding what physically *grounds* it. Everything we experience in a given moment is physically contained within these electrical signals.

Given that the brain physically generates these electrical signals, it stands to reason that the experiences we can have in the present moment are *limited* by what the brain is capable of producing. We cannot experience anything that the brain is not physically able to generate.

WHAT IS THE SELF?

It can be difficult to pinpoint the fundamental characteristics of the self, even though we clearly rely on some notion of it all the time. After all, we constantly use the word "I" and easily distinguish ourselves from other people and objects.

For me, the fundamental nature of the self becomes clearer when

I articulate it in terms of the moment. That is, the self can be understood as the biological entity within each moment that we directly control with our thoughts. We don't have this kind of direct control over other biological entities (such as other humans or animals) or non-biological entities (such as rocks or water).

We not only directly control this biological entity with our thoughts, but we also *directly observe everything it senses, feels, and thinks* in the present moment. We *experience* this biological entity in terms of its sensations, feelings, and thoughts.

What this fundamentally means is that the *self is an experience*. At any given point in time, the self is simply a composite of all the sensorial, emotional, and conceptual experiences it is having in that instant. The self can also be described as an "experience that has become self-aware". An experience that recognizes it is an experience.

Viewing the self as an experience also allows us to identify its three main "parts": the part that *senses*, the part that *feels*, and the part that *thinks*. When referring to the "self", we are typically referring to one or more of these parts.

We can pinpoint other fundamental characteristics of the self when we articulate it in other terms.

Articulating the Self in Terms of What It Wants

In my view, there are two types of wants:

- Fundamental want: Something we desire for its own sake. We don't want it because it will help us get to some other want. It is an end goal.
- Instrumental want: It is not something we desire for its own sake. We only want it because it will eventually get us to a fundamental want. It is a stepping stone toward something else.

What we *fundamentally want* is to optimize our well-being. This core desire can be expressed as two specific fundamental wants:

- To attain sensorial and emotional *satisfaction*.
- To avoid sensorial and emotional *suffering*.

I characterize these as fundamental wants because these are end goals in themselves. They are not steps towards some other objective.

As just mentioned, our instrumental wants help us get to our fundamental wants. They are the physical and mental activities we can do that help us attain enjoyment and avoid anguish. This includes playing sports, catching up with friends, and going for a swim at the beach.

The self is biologically compelled to try to understand how to meet these fundamental wants. That is, to identify what brings us enjoyment and causes us pain. This involves us:

- Learning the specific types of sensorial and emotional gratification we fundamentally want to attain, and which specific physical and mental pursuits will help us do that.
- Learning the specific types of sensorial and emotional distress we fundamentally want to avoid, and which specific physical and mental pursuits keep us from experiencing it.

As mentioned earlier, we tend to comprehend quite well what brings about sensorial enjoyment and pain, but we're far less clear when it comes to emotional experiences. We often try different physical and mental pursuits to increase our contentment, but when they don't seem to work, we usually blame the activity itself, assuming it just isn't inherently satisfying. In reality, the issue is often our mindset. We may lack the mentality that allows us to deeply engage with the experience.

For an activity to become emotionally satisfying, we need to unlearn the mental frameworks that block our contentment and generate distress. We also need to develop a coherent enough model of reality. When we remove the interference that disrupts the playful mind, a wide range of physical and mental pursuits become more emotionally rewarding. As we become more open to different experiences, we find ourselves drawing satisfaction from a broader variety of them.

When we recognize that our fundamental desire is to optimize our satisfaction, we gain a stronger sense of orientation. We're better able to see where we stand in relation to this core aim. Like having a map that shows us where we are and where we're heading. Even a broad recognition of this goal can create a meaningful sense of direction. And this clarity deepens as we begin to figure out:

- The *specific details* of what we fundamentally want. That is, the specific types of sensorial and emotional gratification we desire, and the specific types of sensorial and emotional pain we wish to avoid.
- The *specific* physical and mental undertakings that can help us get the types of enjoyment we're after.
- The *specific* physical and mental undertakings we should avoid as they lead us to sensorial or emotional pain.

Articulating the Self in Terms of the "Present Self", "Past Self", and "Future Self"

We can understand the self more by also articulating it in terms of the "present self", "past self", and "future self".

Every moment in a lifetime is occupied by a particular version of the self. The present moment is occupied by the "present self". Every past moment was occupied by a "past self". Every future moment will be occupied by a "future self". While there is always one present self, there are typically multiple past selves and multiple future selves.

Each version of the self at every single point in time is *utterly unique* to one another. This is because each self experiences a combination of sensations, feelings, and thoughts that no other self before has experienced exactly and that no other self will after. While different versions of the self may go through similar sensations, emotions, and thoughts, the precise combination is never identical. It's not just that the present self differs from past and future selves; every past self is also different from every other past self, and the same goes for future selves. Each version of the self exists only once — in the moment it's generated — and never again.

Strictly speaking, the *only version of the self* that exists at any given moment is the present self. This is because only the present moment exists right now. Past and future moments do not exist in the present, and therefore neither do past or future selves. When the present self thinks about past selves, it is recalling memories that have persisted into the present. These past selves exist only as memories. Likewise, when the present self thinks about future selves, it is imagining hypothetical versions based on present behavior and memories of past selves. It is only as hypotheticals that these future selves exist currently.

Why the Present Self Has a Skewed Impression of the Past Selves' Satisfaction

How the present self *views* its memories of past selves can significantly affect its current level of satisfaction. When it applies specific mental frameworks to these memories, they can become triggers of emotional distress. In other words, recalling the memory causes the present self to experience emotional suffering. These harmful thought patterns were discussed in Chapter 2; they relate to our self-worth, the ego's attachment to specific forms of power, and happiness conditional statements. When the present self disassembles these mental frameworks and stops applying them, its memories shift from being sources of emotional suffering to sources of peace. Its relationship with the past becomes more tranquil. The more the present self makes peace with its memories, the less it suffers. And the more easily it can keep its attention focused on the here and now.

The present self also tends to *underestimate* how many moments of happiness and satisfaction their past selves had. Our minds seem more attentive to picking up on memories of emotional pain. As a result, it's hard for us to even see the memories that can provide us with emotional gratification. As discussed in Chapter 3, I believe our attention is geared this way primarily because of our survival instinct and ego, both of which are trying to figure out how to protect us from future emotional pain. Unfortunately, these aspects of us may push us to keep recalling the memory beyond the point of usefulness, simply because there remains a possibility that valuable information could still be gleaned. As per Chapter 3, we can stop recalling such a memory by convincing the survival-driven and egotistic parts of ourselves that holding onto it for too long undermines our survival and makes us look more foolish.

It's important to recognize that we often underestimate how many moments of happiness and satisfaction our past selves actually experienced. When we leave unchallenged the belief that our past selves weren't happy or satisfied, it can lead to unnecessary feelings of despair. These feelings are a reaction to inaccurate information.

Even when we recall memories that provide emotional gratification, we may find they offer only a little. This might lead our present self to think that when these past events originally happened, they weren't that emotionally satisfying to begin with. Our present self may then conclude that our previous selves lacked happiness or satisfaction. This is a belief that can give rise to despair today. But this despair is unnecessary, as it rests on a faulty assumption: that our memories *reliably* reflect how happy or satisfied we actually were in the past.

While this may seem obvious, we often forget it: the satisfaction we feel while doing something is not the same as when we later recall it. For example, the enjoyment we experience during a concert is different from the feeling we get when remembering it. For whatever reason, the emotional gratification we experience during the event is not perfectly stored in the brain along with the memory. When we recall it, we tend to feel a more subdued version of that gratification. Our brain seems unreliable when it comes to recalling the actual levels of emotional enjoyment our past selves experienced. For this reason, we should be even more inclined to think that the present self is underestimating how happy and satisfied the past selves were. Rather than expecting memories to deliver intense gratification, we should generally expect a more subtle experience.

What might explain why the brain doesn't perfectly store how emotionally satisfying something felt at the time? This is speculative on my part, but it may be that the brain evolved this way as a survival mechanism. Imagine if we could vividly re-experience the full emotional intensity of our happiest memories. We might end up spending much of our time reliving the past simply because it feels so gratifying. That could make us less attentive to the present and more vulnerable to immediate dangers. Our ancestors, if absorbed in emotionally rich memories, might have lost the drive to explore new areas or seek out additional resources critical for survival. In this light, the dulling of emotional intensity in memory might serve as a kind of self-preserving filter, nudging us to stay focused on the here and now.

Can We Arrive at a Complete Understanding of Ourselves?

No, I don't think so. We're too psychologically complex to learn about ourselves in complete detail. It's not possible to grasp everything there is. Instead, what we can do is arrive at an understanding of what we *fundamentally* are. In other words, we should try to grasp the baseline definition of the self. Once we've done that, we can then begin to gather the more *specific details* of who we are.

What one considers to be the "baseline self" may differ from person to person. For me, it includes much of what has already been discussed in this section. Namely:

- *The self is an experience.* There is a part of the self that senses, a part that feels, and a part that thinks.
- The self fundamentally wants to optimize its well-being. As in, attain sensorial and emotional enjoyment and avoid

sensorial and emotional distress. The details to figure out here are the specific types of enjoyment we desire and the specific types of pain we wish to avoid. It is important we also identify which specific physical and mental experiences will gratify us and which cause us to suffer.

- The self can be articulated in terms of the "present self", "past self", and "future self". Each version of the self is utterly unique when compared to one another in terms of their sensations, emotions, and thoughts. Only the present self ever exists at any point in time.

Another component of the baseline self would be our sense of right and wrong. This involves identifying what our core principles are, and then working through the details of how they apply to specific situations. This will be more closely examined in Chapter 6.

While we cannot arrive at a complete view of ourselves, can we at least *prove* that what we do understand aligns with the true self? No, we cannot. We can form an understanding of the self that we *honestly believe* to be true, based on its appearing logically consistent with our observed experiences to date. However, we cannot know or prove it, since we can never rule out the possibility of an unobserved experience contradicting it. Our self-understanding may well be correct, but we can never be certain. We must always allow for the possibility that we are wrong.

6

———

HOW WE UNDERSTAND
WHAT IS RIGHT AND WRONG

Why should we understand this? There are a couple of reasons.

First, our sense of right and wrong is a fundamental building block we need to grasp in sufficient detail before we can consider our model of reality coherent enough. When we gain this understanding, it becomes much easier to relax and enter the playful mind in the present.

Secondly, acting consistently — or not — with our sense of right and wrong can significantly impact our levels of emotional satisfaction. Doing the right thing makes it much easier to like, respect, and be at peace with ourselves. This, in turn, makes it easier to generate happiness. Doing the wrong thing, on the other hand, makes it much harder to feel satisfied with ourselves and to find contentment. The better we recognize which actions feel moral or immoral to us, the more likely we are to feel satisfied and suffer less.

THE GENERAL PROCESS BY WHICH WE UNDERSTAND WHAT IS RIGHT AND WRONG

So how do we come to understand what is moral and immoral? We rely on our conscience to tell us. Our conscience is our brain's sense of right and wrong. This "sense of right and wrong" comprises principles that are embedded in our conscience.

There are two types of principles.

A "general principle" stipulates the reason *why* an action would be considered right or wrong. An example of a general principle is "we should treat others as we would like to be treated". This particular example is often referred to as the golden rule. According to the golden rule, an action is considered immoral if we wouldn't want it done to us.

An "applied principle" is an *application* of a general principle in specific situations. It stipulates which actions would be considered right or wrong in those particular contexts. For example, when applying the golden rule to specific situations, we might develop an applied principle such as "deceiving others is wrong because we would not want that done to us".

How Do These Principles Get Embedded in Our Conscience?

Where do they come from?

One might think that all the principles currently held in our conscience were taught to us by our parents and broader society during childhood. While they may have taught us many of these ethics, I don't believe they are responsible for all the ones we now hold.

We encounter many situations in life that involve some form of moral consideration, even from a young age. It seems highly unlikely that our parents and broader society managed to pass on principles that covered every single situation we faced. Perhaps the ethics they conveyed addressed the vast majority, but it wouldn't have been literally all of them.

So what did we do when we encountered a situation for which no previously taught rule seemed to apply? Our conscience would formulate its own principle *independently*. It had to devise some kind of internal guidance to help us judge which action was right and which was wrong in this scenario. But how could our conscience come up with such guidance? Where did it come from? This capacity for "independent moral thinking" must arise from the physical structure of our brain. That is, our brain must be biologically predisposed to have our conscience generate specific principles in response to particular situations. This independent moral thinking is also what we might refer to as our "moral instinct" or "moral intuition".

Another important point is that we didn't accept every rule taught to us by our parents and broader society. Perhaps in early childhood, we did, and so everything conveyed to us during that stage became embedded in our conscience. But as we got older, our brain physically developed the capacity to formulate principles on its own. Our moral intuition grew stronger. With this ability to think independently about what is ethical, our conscience could begin to disagree with and even reject new rules introduced by others. The principle held in our conscience could then be one we had formulated independently, rather than one someone else was trying to instill.

Our conscience could also come to disagree with and reject principles that had been taught earlier and were already embedded. It would no longer retain these rules; instead, it would replace them with ones it had formed on its own. As our brains continued to develop the capacity for independent moral thinking, our conscience became increasingly able to reject guidance taught by others; whether newly introduced or carried over from the past.

There can be cases where our conscience agrees more with a new principle taught by someone else over its own independent formulation. In such instances, our internally developed rule will no longer remain embedded in our conscience, while the newly taught principle will take its place.

To summarize the above, the principles embedded in our

conscience today are shaped by a *combination* of what we've been taught and the biological structure of our brain.

THE HIDDEN PRINCIPLES OF OUR CONSCIENCE

When a principle becomes part of our conscience, we may become consciously aware of it. One sign of this awareness is when we articulate the principle in words. For example, most of us have expressed support for the idea of "treating others as we would like to be treated". This suggests we're highly aware that our moral compass holds this value.

However, our conscious mind isn't fully aware of all the rules that make up our moral framework. Some were embedded through the *subconscious*, without ever entering our high-level awareness. This can happen in two ways.

One way is when someone teaches us a new principle that we weren't explicitly paying close attention to, but our subconscious takes note of it. The subconscious then embeds the guidance into our moral compass. It may have briefly entered our high-level awareness during the discussion, but didn't remain there.

Another way is when our conscience independently formulates a new rule in response to a situation, but this formulation is never explicitly articulated in our high-level awareness. It happens subconsciously in the background.

How Does the Conscious Mind Detect a Subconsciously Embedded Principle?

This awareness arises when we encounter a situation that "tests" the principle embedded in our subconscious. In such moments, our conscience evaluates which actions would be right or wrong under this guidance. During that evaluation, the principle may surface into conscious awareness, allowing us to articulate it in words.

For example, suppose someone asks us to lie on their behalf to help them avoid consequences. We instinctively feel uneasy, even though we've never explicitly considered our stance on lying for others. As we reflect, we might think, "I don't believe it's right to lie for someone, even if I care about them". In this case, the situation tested a rule that had been subconsciously embedded. And the process of grappling with the dilemma brought that principle to the surface.

There are situations that test a subconsciously embedded rule, but its articulation doesn't always surface readily in our high-level awareness. Even so, our conscious mind can still *infer* what this hidden principle might be; especially when our conscience produces *strong feelings of right or wrong* in response. These emotional reactions serve as clues, pointing us toward the under-lying value our mind is operating from, even if we haven't yet expressed it in words.

When our moral compass approves of an action because it aligns with an embedded rule, our conscience can generate a feeling that the action is right. Conversely, when our conscience disapproves of an action because it conflicts with an embedded value, it produces a feeling that the action is wrong. When these moral feelings are particularly strong, they rise into our high-level awareness. In such moments, we might think, "Action A *feels* right" and "Action B *feels* wrong".

Let's return to the example where we've been asked to lie on someone else's behalf. Even if we can't immediately articulate the underlying rule, we may still feel strong emotional discomfort at the thought of lying. This discomfort signals that a principle — such as "it's wrong to mislead, even for someone we care about" — is being activated within our moral compass, even if it hasn't yet been consciously expressed. When our mind detects these strong feelings of right and wrong trying to guide our behavior, we often refer to them as the "little voice in the back of the head". From these moral feelings, our awareness can work backward and infer the general principle explaining why one action feels right and the other feels wrong. By reflecting on the feeling, we can then reverse-engineer the rule that had been operating in the background.

Is There a Chance We Could Make a Mistake While Reverse-Engineering the General Principle?

As in, we might articulate the rule in a way that differs significantly from what's actually embedded in our moral compass? The answer is yes. The difficulty comes from the process: our conscious mind attempts to reverse-engineer the general principle based solely on how it interprets the feelings of right and wrong it detects — and those *interpretations aren't always reliable*.

For instance, we may find ourselves in a situation where our moral compass disapproves of an action and evokes a feeling that it is wrong. But our conscious mind might misinterpret that moral signal and conclude that "this action feels right". Returning to the example of someone asking us to lie on their behalf: if our conscience produces only a subtle feeling of discomfort, we might misread it as approval. We may then try to reverse-engineer a general principle like "it's acceptable to lie for someone you care about", even though this doesn't accurately reflect our moral compass. Our interpretation of these moral feelings tends to be more reliable when the signals are strong and distinct. But when they're faint, conflicted, or ambiguous, the chances of misinterpretation increase.

These moral feelings become especially hard to interpret accurately when the brain is *simultaneously generating other strong emotions* that don't originate from the conscience. For example, our ego might produce feelings of powerlessness, helplessness, or anger. These intense emotions create "noise", making it harder for us to hear the quieter signals of right and wrong coming from our moral compass.

When such egotistic feelings are present, they can drive someone to inflict suffering or harm on others — even though such actions conflict with their moral compass. This emotional noise can lead the conscious mind to mistake the ego's intense distress for a strong moral impulse — a false sense that the action is right — even though their moral compass is signaling otherwise. By unlearning the mental frameworks that generate this noise, we make it easier for our conscious mind to detect the genuine signals of right and wrong coming from our deeper moral framework. As we dismantle these egotistic thought patterns, the feelings of powerlessness, helplessness, and anger begin to fade.

Now that we're aware of the factors that can lead to an unreliable interpretation of our moral feelings, we're better positioned to recognize them when they are present. If our moral intuitions feel vague, or if other strong emotions unrelated to our conscience are generating noise, we can take extra care in interpreting these signals. Simply being more attentive can improve our interpretation's reliability and the alignment between the general principle we reverse-engineer and our deeper values.

Can We Ever Be 100% Certain That We Are Accurately Interpreting Our Moral Intuitions?

No, we can never be 100% certain. Even when our moral feelings are strong and there's little to no emotional noise, the accuracy of our interpretation may be higher. But complete certainty is still out of reach. We can believe that our interpretation is accurate, yet we must always remain open to the possibility that it isn't.

I mention all this because many of us rely heavily on our moral feelings when trying to identify which rules are embedded in our conscience. Yet many don't fully consider the possibility that they might be misinterpreting their moral compass. I'm not suggesting we shouldn't rely on these feelings; rather, we should do so with care. I'm also not suggesting we should seriously doubt whether the ethics we've articulated genuinely reflect our moral compass. I'm only suggesting that we remain mindful of the possibility that they don't.

As we improve at interpreting our moral feelings, we may discover that some of our stated values don't accurately represent our conscience. For instance, we may claim as a principle that lying on other's behalf is morally acceptable, yet feel a strong aversion to it. In such moments, we should be honest with ourselves and consciously acknowledge the misalignment. That way, we can revise or replace the stated rule with one that genuinely reflects the values held by our conscience.

It can be difficult to consciously accept that we've been following an inaccurate rule, as doing so may trigger destabilizing emotions. When we have enough mental fortitude to withstand this discomfort, we're more likely to be honest about the inaccuracy. But when our mental resilience falls short, it becomes harder to admit that our conscience no longer supports the principle — or perhaps never did. These unsettling emotions can grow so intense that we suppress — or willfully misinterpret — our moral intuitions.

Is It Necessary to Be Aware of All Our Inner Principles?

In my view, no. I believe it's enough to be consciously aware of the general values that matter most to our conscience. We can gauge a principle's importance by how strongly it affects our ability to like, respect, and feel at peace with ourselves. When we act against a deeply held rule, the resulting deterioration in our emotional state is usually much greater than when we go against a less significant one.

The general principle that matters most to me — and that I believe many of us share deep down — is the golden rule: treat others as we would like to be treated. What makes this rule especially valuable is its ability to provide clear moral guidance in most situations we encounter. At its core, it simply asks us to consider one basic question before acting: would it be wrong if someone did this to me?

This usually makes it straightforward to apply. For instance, most of us wouldn't want to be lied to, stolen from, or physically harmed. So, under the golden rule, these actions would typically be seen as immoral, regardless of whether we're the ones doing them or someone else is. While we may still need other principles for more specific or unusual cases, I find it reassuring that a single rule can guide the vast majority of our moral decisions.

WHAT DOES IT MEAN TO BE A "GOOD PERSON"?

Every person experiences impulses to do *both* the right thing and the wrong thing. No one only feels the urge to do what is right, just as no one only feels the urge to do what is wrong. In my view, what fundamentally distinguishes a good person from a bad one is which type of impulse tends to be stronger overall.

I consider a good person to be someone who generally has a stronger impulse to act in line with their conscience. By "generally", I mean that the urge to do the right thing tends to be stronger in *most situations*, but not necessarily in all. There may still be circumstances where the impulse to behave immorally is stronger. For this reason, when I call someone "good", I'm not suggesting they're entirely good or free of bad impulses. As mentioned, I see everyone as a mixture of both. It's just that this person tends to lean more toward acting ethically than not.

Likewise, I would consider a bad person to be someone who generally has a stronger urge to act inconsistently with their moral compass. That is, they tend to feel a stronger impulse to behave unethically in most scenarios, though not always. There may still be some situations where their impulse to do the right thing is stronger. As you might guess, when I call someone "bad", I'm not suggesting they're entirely that way or devoid of good impulses. Again, everyone is a mixture of both. It's just that this person happens to be more bad than good.

We'll now examine two key traits that strongly contribute to a person being more good than bad.

The Trait of High Mental Fortitude

A person with high mental fortitude can more easily accept when they've articulated a rule that inaccurately reflects their moral compass. They can then take steps to replace it with something more aligned. This same fortitude also helps them accept that they have the *capacity* to behave unethically. And it's precisely because they acknowledge this that they're able to manage their impulses and choose to do what is right.

The Trait of Effectively Managing One's Impulses

This involves being effective at weakening the impulse to act immorally while strengthening the impulse to act morally.

A person can weaken an immoral urge by dismantling the thought patterns that give rise to it in the first place. This includes any mistaken belief that the action will lead to happiness, as well as any mental frameworks that create a desire to take out their pain on someone else. Dismantling the latter is part of managing the ego, as discussed in Chapter 2.

A person can strengthen the moral impulse by remembering that such actions help them like, respect, and be at peace with themselves. By doing so, they can *weigh* whatever perceived benefit they might gain from acting unethically against the emotional consequences of such behavior.

When they weigh things up, a person who leans toward goodness is unlikely to believe that this benefit is worth making it harder to like, respect, and be at peace with themselves. They will usually conclude that, while acting morally may be difficult at times, it ultimately serves their happiness better than doing what's immoral. They will recognize that doing what is right will help them be more satisfied in the ways that matter most to them. They will be able to live with themselves a lot easier.

Why Someone Lacking These Traits Is More Likely to Be Bad Than Good

A person who is "more bad than good" tends to display the opposite traits. Rather than being strongly self-honest, they are often self-deceptive. This shows up in a several key ways. For instance, they may resist acknowledging when they've followed a value that doesn't actually reflect their moral compass.

They also deceive themselves into believing they lack the capacity, impulse, or desire to do the wrong thing. Even when they feel the urge to act immorally, they convince themselves that the action isn't actually unethical. As discussed in Chapter 2, they often generate a justification that supposedly cancels out the wrongness of the behavior. However, this reasoning is usually a form of self-deception they don't fully believe. They do this because being honest about the action's immorality would make it harder to go through with it. To avoid that internal conflict, they ignore what their moral compass is telling them, choosing instead to suppress or distort their moral intuitions. Ultimately, they want to claim whatever benefit they believe the immoral action will bring.

Another reason they deceive themselves about their immoral behavior is to avoid the emotional consequences of acting against their moral compass. As discussed in Chapter 2, this self-deception operates only at the conscious level. Their subconscious still recognizes the inconsistency, which means they continue to experience the emotional fallout. These emotions may be suppressed, but they still feel some form of disappointment, shame, or self-hatred. So despite whatever justification they use to excuse the behavior — and despite whatever benefit they hoped to gain — they are no closer to being happy. It's actually a bit further away now.

This self-deceiving quality is why such a person often lacks another trait that is vital to being more good: the ability to effectively manage their impulses. After all, if they don't think the action they're considering is wrong, why would they bother controlling the impulse behind it? As a result, they take no steps to dismantle the thought patterns that fuel the immoral urge. They don't question any false beliefs that the action will bring them happiness, nor do they challenge the egotistic mental frameworks that drive their desire to inflict suffering on others.

They also don't bother to weigh the perceived benefit of the action against its emotional consequences, since they see no need to strengthen their moral impulse. This ease of self-deception is why so many of us act inconsistently with the golden rule. This is despite its presence across many cultures in various forms for thousands of years, and its deep roots in most people's moral compass.

To be clear, a good person isn't always honest with themselves or consistently in control of their impulses, but they usually are. A bad person, by contrast, tends to be more dishonest than honest and more impulsive than restrained. What I am highlighting here again is that good and bad people share the same fundamental traits. What sets them apart is the extent to which those traits are developed. One leans more toward qualities that foster goodness; the other, toward those that hinder it. If a person wants to improve their moral behavior — moving from "bad" to "good", or from "good" to "better" — they need to keep strengthening the key traits that lead them in that direction.

What ultimately separates a good person from a bad one is their *understanding* of how to develop the traits of self-honesty and impulse control. Those who grasp how to strengthen these qualities can become "more good", while those who lack this awareness cannot. Quite simply, people who don't understand how to improve themselves are unable to do so. When I describe someone as a "bad person", I don't mean they want to be bad. I believe they ultimately want to be good, but they're afraid of what that requires. They're afraid to face the immoral aspects of themselves, and too afraid to change.

Why We Should Be Honest with Ourselves When We Do Something Immoral

If we're going to do the wrong thing, we shouldn't deceive ourselves about it. We should be honest enough to consciously acknowledge that the action is wrong, either at the time we do it or soon after. This kind of self-honesty allows us to retain at least some respect for who we are. But when we lie to ourselves instead, we make fools of ourselves. That's exactly the kind of fool we should avoid becoming.

To support greater self-honesty, I want to challenge a common justification people often use to excuse behaving unethically: the claim that the action is *necessary* to reach a particular goal. In my view, this rationale is usually a form of self-deception. There are three main problems with this excuse.

First, deep down, the same people would likely view the action as wrong if someone else did it to them using the same reasoning.

Second, for an action to be essential to meeting an objective, there must be no alternative course of action available. But have we actually exhausted all other options? If not, then the action isn't necessary, it's simply more convenient.

Third, even if an ordinarily immoral action is genuinely required to attain an objective, we should still ask: is the goal itself genuinely necessary? If the goal is to feed ourselves so we don't die, I can somewhat understand resorting to theft, provided there are no other options available. But if the goal is to get a promotion at work — and not related to our physical survival — I don't see how we could justify resorting to lying or manipulation, even if we believe it's necessary in that particular work environment. In other words, if we're not going to die or suffer serious harm by not attaining the objective, it's hard to argue that it's essential. And if the objective isn't essential, then neither is taking a morally wrong action to meet it.

WHY IS IT SO HARD FOR SOME PEOPLE TO ACCEPT THEIR CAPACITY TO ACT IMMORALLY?

As discussed in Chapter 2, when someone wrongs us and our ego is attached to the power to prevent it, we often experience feelings of powerlessness, helplessness, and anger. In response to this distress, we tend to direct our anger not only at the person who committed the act, but also at the qualities within them that made it possible. In other words, we hate that they had the capability, the impulse, and the desire to do the wrong thing.

For as long as we continue to hate these qualities in others, we can't help but hate those same qualities within ourselves. Some might argue that this self-hatred is ultimately useful, as it increases the likelihood we'll do the right thing. In other words, we'll choose what's right to avoid the self-hatred that follows doing what's wrong.

While I agree that self-hatred can serve a purpose, if it becomes too *intense*, it can backfire and lead us to do the wrong thing more often, not less. When the self-hatred we feel toward immoral traits is overwhelming, it creates a strong incentive to deny that the action we're considering is wrong. We deceive ourselves into believing we have a justification that cancels out its immorality. By pretending the action is acceptable, we avoid consciously confronting our own capacity to do harm. In doing so, we spare ourselves from the self-hatred we would otherwise feel for possessing those qualities.

Of course, consciously denying that we carry these traits doesn't actually spare us from intense self-hatred. The subconscious still recognizes these immoral attributes within us, so the self-hatred remains. Self-deception merely pushes this anguish below the surface, though often not very effectively. The emotional turmoil still finds ways to bleed into consciousness.

By consciously deceiving ourselves into believing an action isn't wrong, we avoid managing the impulse to act against our conscience. Without that management, the urge to do the wrong thing can remain strong, while the impulse to do what's right stays weak. Ironically, intense self-hatred doesn't make it easier to choose the moral path. It can actually make it easier to choose the immoral one. This is why I believe that people who behave immorally often carry deep and intense self-hatred.

To Stop Hating These Traits in Ourselves, We Need to Stop Hating Them in Others

The solution lies in making peace with the wrongs done to us in the past. We do this by dismantling the egotistic mental frameworks that generate feelings of powerlessness, helplessness, and anger. When the emotional pain subsides, it's much easier to make peace with both the wrong actions done to us and the traits that caused them.

As we stop hating these qualities in others, we gradually stop hating them in ourselves. This shift allows us to be more honest with ourselves, enabling us to consciously acknowledge our own capacity for immoral behavior. In turn, we're more likely to stay honest when we feel the urge to do something wrong. Instead of justifying the action through self-deception, we're able to recognize it for what it is and manage the impulse accordingly. This is why I believe people who consistently do the right thing tend to harbor very little hatred toward others. And, as a result, very little hatred toward themselves.

If we only have low levels of hatred for these immoral traits, what will motivate us to act in line with our conscience? As discussed earlier, doing the wrong thing still carries emotional consequences beyond self-hatred; namely, feelings like disappointment and shame. These emotions are unpleasant enough to deter us, but not so overwhelming that we feel the need to pretend an immoral action is acceptable.

In addition, acting against our moral compass can make it harder to like, respect, and be at peace with ourselves. So even with only low levels of hatred toward these traits, we still have strong emotional reasons to do what's right. In the end, acting morally remains far more satisfying than the alternative.

Making peace with the qualities in others that allow them to behave immorally doesn't mean we tolerate being treated unfairly. We may still take steps to prevent such actions, but our motivation won't come from ego or from feelings of powerlessness, helplessness, or anger. Instead, we'll view these measures as practical steps to protect our well-being and interests.

Even after self-hatred fades, a person may still struggle to accept the ongoing presence of their impulse and desire to behave immorally. This struggle can deepen when they realize that these traits can never be fully erased. But just because we can't eliminate this aspect of ourselves entirely doesn't mean we shouldn't work to *minimize* its influence on our behavior. For the most part, I believe we can reduce this impulse and desire to the point where they have only a negligible impact on our decisions. As mentioned above, when we act consistently with our conscience, we tend to feel more satisfied and happier with ourselves than if we did the opposite.

Recognizing the good within us also helps us come to terms with the bad that remains. This means acknowledging our enduring impulse, desire, and capacity to do what is right. These qualities, like their darker counterparts, can never be fully erased. We should get into the habit of seeing both.

Moving On from the Wrong Things We've Done in the Past

It can also be difficult to come to terms with the immoral acts we have done previously. The first thing we often think of is how to undo the wrong action, as if it never happened. But of course, that's impossible. No action we take afterward can truly reverse what happened. We can't erase it from our record, so it's best to let go of that expectation.

What we can do instead is try to make up for it as much as possible. This means taking deliberate steps to become a better person in response. It involves consciously acknowledging that our moral compass has a principle that disapproves of the action — an action we had no valid justification for. "Making up for it" also means putting in consistent effort to manage our impulses so that we're far less likely to repeat the same mistake.

It also helps to make amends, as much as possible, with the person we wronged. While none of this undoes the action — it still remains part of our record — our subsequent behavior can help "balance it out" to some degree. The wrong and the right don't cancel each other out; they co-exist. Just as there will always be bad actions in our past that can't be erased, there will also be good actions that can't be taken away. For example, if we once lied to someone and broke their trust, we can't undo that moment, but we can sincerely apologize, take responsibility, and show through future behavior that we've become more honest and trustworthy. That new pattern doesn't erase the lie, but it does help them and us move on.

Does doing all this mean we've forgiven ourselves? In many cases, yes, but not always. Sometimes the nature of what we did is so difficult to accept that self-forgiveness remains out of reach, no matter how much we try to make amends. Still, that doesn't mean we shouldn't try to become a better person or repair the harm we've caused. These efforts can still somewhat ease the emotional turmoil of acting against our moral compass. While we don't move on completely, we've at least done as much as we can.

When we have the courage to acknowledge our past mistakes and change our behavior, we become more satisfied with ourselves. We gain greater self-respect and feel more at peace with who we are. Even if we can't undo the action or fully forgive ourselves, we can still take steps to reduce the suffering it caused, whether to others or to ourselves. By making peace with what happened as much as possible, we make the mistake easier to emotionally live with.

DO WE ULTIMATELY SEE A PRINCIPLE AS MORE RIGHT WHEN OTHERS AGREE WITH IT?

It might seem that way on the surface, but when we look more closely, I don't believe we do. How "right" we consider a principle to be is determined solely by our conscience — our *individual* sense of right and wrong. Ultimately, we rely on this internal moral compass to guide us in deciding which principles to follow and which to reject.

Whether others agree or disagree with a principle embedded in our conscience has no fundamental impact on how right we perceive that rule to be. If others happen to agree with one of our principles, I don't believe our conscience sees it as "more right" than before. That value would be just as right to us as it always was. Likewise, if others disagree, our conscience doesn't necessarily see it as "less right". The perceived rightness of the rule remains unchanged, because it originates from within.

If other people's agreement or disagreement really changed how right our conscience thought a principle was, then our moral compass would only hold values that society widely accepts. Our conscience wouldn't be capable of holding ethics that fall outside the mainstream. Yet I would wager that almost everyone has rejected at least one, if not several, of the values society appears to advocate. We're able to reject these societal ethics because we ultimately rely on our own individual sense of right and wrong. Even for the values we've adopted from society, whether they remain part of our conscience depends on whether our personal moral sense continues to align with them.

The only thing that should really change how right our conscience considers a principle to be is a *convincing argument*, not a tally of how many people agree or disagree with it. For example, we should see a rule as "more right" not because it has widespread support, but because it aligns more closely with the rest of our ethical framework. Likewise, we should view a principle as "less right" not simply because others reject it, but because it conflicts with our deeper moral values.

Why Do Some People Care Whether a Principle Has Widespread Support?

I think some people seek widespread support for their principles because they've been led to believe they can't rely on their conscience alone to determine what's right. They believe that for their ethics to be valid at all, those principles must *originate* from an external source of morality. For many, this external source is the collective conscience of humanity.

Under this view, if a principle in someone's conscience can't be shown to originate from an external moral source, then it has no grounds for being right. In this framework, any validity a person's principles have comes from being derived from that external source — not from the individual themselves.

I used to share the view that every rule needs to originate from an external source — such as humanity's collective conscience — but I no longer do. That's because, for the vast majority of moral quandaries, we don't find genuinely unanimous support for what the governing principle should be. These differences are obvious across cultures, but they exist even within individual cultures as well. For example, in some societies, individual freedom is treated as a moral cornerstone, while in others, maintaining social harmony is seen as more important, even if that means limiting personal expression. Views on issues like euthanasia, capital punishment, or whether lying is ever morally acceptable also vary widely. Even within a single country, you'll find people fiercely divided on whether abortion is a moral right or a moral wrong. People are often quick to claim that their rule originates from "humanity", but in reality, they've only consulted a relatively small subset of the global population. Usually it's just those who already agree with them.

There are other ways in which people who claim that all their principles originate from an external source don't actually behave that way. In practice, they often rely on their own individual sense of right and wrong, even when no external source supports it. As mentioned earlier, our conscience has the capacity to devise its own principles when faced with situations it hasn't been explicitly taught how to handle. Moreover, our conscience does not automatically accept every principle that is widely endorsed by society. We're capable of rejecting socially accepted norms when they conflict with our internal moral sense. This shows that, in reality, we're not merely trying to derive all our principles from an external source. Even the principles passed down to us by society remain part of our moral framework only so long as our conscience continues to agree with them.

Other External Sources People Try to Rely On for Moral Principles

For those who believe that valid moral principles must originate from an external source, the collective conscience of humanity isn't the only one they turn to. There are two other entities people often rely on: the physical universe itself and what they believe to be its creator, usually some type of god. Each of these comes with its own set of challenges when used as a foundation for morality.

The main challenge in thinking the physical universe has a sense of right and wrong is that we'd have to show it possesses sentience. Without this, it couldn't have a point of view on what is moral or immoral. I don't think it's impossible that such sentience exists, but I don't see how one could adequately demonstrate it. And even if we assume, for the sake of argument, that the universe is sentient and does have a moral perspective, how could we reliably show that we're communicating with it in a way that lets us understand what it thinks? I haven't seen any convincing evidence of that.

The primary challenge with using a deity as a source of moral principles is establishing that such an entity actually exists. While I believe a universal creator is possible, I don't currently hold that belief based on what I've observed so far. That said, I fully allow for the possibility that I could be wrong.

For the sake of argument, let's assume we could adequately demonstrate a sentient universe and that we could understand its moral principles, or that a universal creator exists. Even then, I would still rely on my own individual sense of right and wrong to accept or reject the principles they put forward. For instance, if such an entity commanded me to enslave others or kill in their name and claimed it was morally right, my conscience would not see it that way. Likewise, if they endorsed principles I already agree with, I wouldn't see those rules as any more right than I did before.

Is There a Danger of People Just Choosing Their Own Principles?

In my view, as outlined above, our principles originate from our conscience rather than from external sources. But does this create a problem? The main concern people have is that if our principles come from our individual sense of right and wrong, then anyone could simply *choose* which ones to adopt. And, in doing so, *decide* for themselves what is right and wrong.

This concern is unwarranted because, even though these principles come from within our own minds, we don't actually get to choose them. I can't, for example, simply decide that stealing or murder are right. My brain *compels* my conscience to think that such actions are wrong. I don't get to decide what my conscience considers to be ethical. Usually, it's not about choosing our moral principles; it's about discovering what our conscience already believes is right at that point in time.

The real issue is not people deciding what is right and wrong, but *deceiving* themselves about what their conscience actually thinks. People struggle to admit that their principles have changed, or that some rules they've articulated never truly reflected what was within their conscience. Their resistance to examining whether their rules reflect their moral compass often stems from the destabilizing emotions that would arise if they confronted these internal moral conflicts. They don't have high mental fortitude for that.

Does the notion of an external source of morality help with this problem? It depends on the individual and the nature of their self-deception, but for the most part, I believe it makes the problem worse. People can more easily sustain the self-deception that their stated principles align with their moral compass by claiming those principles come from an external source. This claim allows them to avoid examining their own internal moral conflicts. Throughout history, people have enslaved, killed, and oppressed others while insisting their actions were justified by a divine source. When that external source is removed, so is the assumption that their principles come from something infallible. When they recognize that these rules are coming from themselves, they're more likely to see the human fallibility behind them. And, in turn, become more open to honest self-examination.

If we want to guard against self-deception in moral thinking, we should encourage people to be honest with themselves about the principles that genuinely form their sense of right and wrong. They should also stay honest when those principles change. This kind of self-honesty requires mental fortitude. Only those who are willing to consciously endure the emotional discomfort of moral conflict will be able to examine it.

ARE WE UNDER AN *OBLIGATION* TO DO THE RIGHT THING?

When people believe that only externally derived principles are valid, they tend to view doing the right thing as an "obligation" to that external source.

If we believe instead that our principles originate from our own individual sense of right and wrong, we no longer see ourselves as acting out of obligation to something outside of us. There's no sense of an external force being imposed on us. However, within this view, we can still regard ourselves as acting out of obligation, but it's an obligation we place on ourselves. It's one imposed by our own conscience.

That said, I don't believe we need to see ourselves as acting under obligation in order to do what's right. I don't choose the right action because I feel I owe it to myself or to someone else. I do it because it helps me like, respect, and be at peace with myself. It serves my happiness better. I'm always free to do the wrong thing. I just don't do it, or at least I try not to, because it doesn't lead to the kind of happiness I want.

7

A DEFINITION OF LIFE THAT ENCAPSULATES OUR EXPERIENCES

Why arrive at a definition of life? As a reminder, life is a foundational building block we need to understand in sufficient detail for our model of reality to be coherent. When we gain a deep enough understanding of what life is, we become less preoccupied with existential questions and more engaged with the present. Our mind becomes more playful and open toward what is happening right in front of us.

THE SEARCH FOR A DEFINITION OF LIFE WE HONESTLY BELIEVE IN

When trying to arrive at a definition of life, we seek one that we *honestly believe* aligns logically with our observed experiences. In theory, we should be rejecting conceptions we believe have been contradicted by what we have observed. Yet at times, we may even reject a definition we still regard as logically consistent; especially if we have been conditioned to accept only what can be proven true with 100% certainty.

As discussed in Chapter 4, we cannot prove any understanding with 100% certainty because we can't rule out the possibility that it could be contradicted by something we haven't observed. This means no definition of life we have can ever be proven true. Even if we arrive at a conception we genuinely believe is logically consistent with our observations, the possibility of contradiction still remains. We can honestly believe this conception is correct, but we cannot prove that it is. If we've been conditioned to accept only what can be proven with 100% certainty, we should challenge that way of thinking. Otherwise, we risk rejecting conceptions of life that are actually consistent with our observations.

There's another way of thinking we may have been conditioned into; one that can also interfere with our ability to arrive at a definition of life that makes sense given our experiences. It is the view that life is defined as the pursuit of one thing. People conditioned in this way believe that identifying that one thing will unlock a comprehensive understanding of what life is about. The problem with this way of thinking is that it *reduces life* to a single pursuit, excluding all other experiences.

In my view, life is about much more than just one aim. Trying to define it this way — while leaving out everything else we've experienced — results in a definition that is both incomplete and inconsistent with what we've observed. The many experiences that fall outside that one pursuit are undeniably part of life and should be part of our definition somehow. If we've been conditioned to think otherwise, we should challenge it so we can arrive at a view of life that is more complete and more consistent with our experiences.

A Definition of Life Rooted in How We Experience It

This is a definition I believe to be logically consistent with our observed experiences: "Life is the sensorial, emotional, and conceptual experience of biologically existing in each moment". To me, this conception, though brief, encapsulates the fundamental qualities of life. These qualities become more apparent when we elaborate on the three components that make up the definition:

"Life is the sensorial, emotional, conceptual experience...": Here, life is framed fundamentally as an *experience*. And every experience we observe — whether it be sensorial, emotional, or conceptual — is part of it. No experience we have is excluded from this definition of life. Another way to look at this is that the answer to life isn't made up of *thoughts* alone. It also includes our *sensations* and *feelings*. We often think of life's answer as something we arrive at purely through thought, but it becomes much more complete when we extend it to these other forms of experience.

"...of biologically existing...": This refers to how the experience of life arises from the biological processes of a living being. As discussed in Chapter 5, our sensorial, emotional, and conceptual experiences are generated by the brain through electrical signals. Since our bodies are *constantly* undergoing these biological processes, we keep generating these electrical signals, and hence, the experience of life continues.

"...in each moment": This refers to how we always experience life through the sensations, emotions, and thoughts contained within a given moment. At any point in time, our experience of life is bound within the limits of that single instant.

What we've discussed so far represents what I consider the most basic definition of life. However, other ways of defining life still need to be explored and clarified before we can fully move beyond our preoccupation with its conception. I'd wager that most of us have considered these other avenues to some extent, but haven't followed them through to their logical conclusions. It's this unresolved thinking that keeps drawing our minds back to these questions. The rest of this chapter will present the conclusions I honestly believe to be true.

ANOTHER ISSUE WITH DEFINING LIFE AS THE PURSUIT OF ONE THING

Conceiving of life as the pursuit of a single thing is not only reductive, but it can also limit our capacity for satisfaction in many ways.

Letting go of this narrow view opens us up to deeper and more varied forms of satisfaction.

Firstly, as mentioned earlier, this definition implies that only one thing matters, and everything else does not. As discussed in Chapter 1, our ability to engage with and find enjoyment in something is often shaped by how important we believe it to be. If we think that only one thing matters — for example, winning a tennis competition — we'll feel engaged and satisfied only when we're pursuing that specific goal. If we regard everything else — anything unrelated to winning this competition — as unimportant, we will find it difficult to engage sincerely with those other aspects of life. As a result, it will be hard to take part in them and experience genuine contentment. When we move away from this reductive definition, we begin to see more things as important and can engage with them more fully.

Secondly, this narrow conceptualization can lead us to structure our entire life around a single pursuit. We may try to dedicate each moment to getting closer to that one goal. Life, instead of being about many things, becomes about just this. Even if we succeed in organizing our life this way, it will likely feel incomplete because we've excluded everything else. By letting go of this simplistic definition, we open ourselves to a broader range of experiences. This allows for a greater sense of wholeness, even if we can't do absolutely everything.

Thirdly, when we structure our life around a single pursuit, we may start to measure each moment by how well it serves that goal. We begin to value the moments that help us move closer to it, while dismissing those that don't. For example, we might appreciate the time we use to train for competitive tennis, yet overlook the moments spent doing anything unrelated.

By constantly evaluating our experience through the lens of progress toward one objective, we stop seeing each moment as something to be explored and appreciated for its own sake. Instead of focusing on the present and freely discovering it as it unfolds, we become preoccupied with how it is serving something else. We should be able to go for a jog on the beach and simply enjoy it, without thinking about how the fitness might benefit our tennis game later. When we stop using this reductive definition, we are better able to explore each point in time free from such measures.

The reason we're so willing to accept this narrow conceptualization is that we desire simplicity. When we have one clear aim — instead of many — it simplifies our decision-making, as we can direct every action toward that single goal. We take comfort in this straightforwardness. However, to insist that life can be reduced to one thing is an *oversimplification* that misrepresents what life is.

HOW MANY MOMENTS MAKE UP A SINGLE LIFE?

When we think of life, we usually think of it as all the moments that occur from birth to death. As we move from one moment to the next, we still occupy the same life.

I am predisposed to look at life a bit differently. I think that each moment is its own self-contained life. We *experience* the entirety of one life in each moment. As we move from one moment to the next, we also move from one life to the next. Overall, what this means is that instead of having only one life, we have multiple lives. Seen this way, each instance of life we experience is utterly unique, as the precise combination of sensations, feelings, and thoughts within each moment never repeats. Each new instance is occupied by a unique self shaped by that one-of-a-kind experiential mix.

How Seeing Each Moment as a New Life Can Reduce Suffering

When a particularly undesirable event occurs, we may frame it as having "ruined" or "tarnished" our life. This kind of framing often leads to disappointment and regret. On top of that, we may apply mental frameworks that cause us to suffer even more emotionally. Below are some common examples:

- Our ego cares about the power to prevent our life overall from being tarnished or ruined by particularly undesirable events. When that power feels lost, we may experience emotions like powerlessness, helplessness, and anger.

- We adopt a conditional belief about happiness: that if our life overall is tarnished or ruined by a particularly undesirable event, then happiness becomes impossible. This belief can lead to despair.

It's easier to believe our entire life has been tarnished or ruined — and to adopt harmful mental frameworks — when we think of ourselves as having only one life. It is much harder for us to think this when we see every moment as its own self-contained life and that we can begin again with the next life in the next moment. With this mindset, every moment becomes a chance to start over. We might think that *some of our lives* have been tarnished or ruined by the undesirable event, but we regard this "effect" as confined to those particular lives in those moments. All our remaining lives across all subsequent moments can remain untarnished. By viewing life in this way, we are a lot less likely to emotionally suffer; and if we do suffer, it is not nearly as much.

Regardless of whether we see ourselves as having just one life or many, we should dismantle the mental frameworks above. As a reminder, it's not the undesirable event that causes emotional pain, but the frameworks we apply to it. Two people can face the same event, yet only one suffers because only one adopts these thought patterns. The core techniques for undoing them were discussed in Chapter 2.

If we see ourselves as having only one life, and we believe it has been ruined, we need to challenge that framing. Yes, the event may have affected our life in some way, but has it truly *tarnished* or *ruined* it? Do we even understand what it would mean for a life to warrant such labels? Have we logically demonstrated that our life has reached such a state, or have we simply *assumed* it has? Our life may be worse in some ways because of the event — but is it worse in *all* ways?

Just because something deeply undesirable happens doesn't mean a tarnished or ruined life is the inevitable consequence. The undesirable event is the cost of doing business, but does it have to spoil everything else life has to offer? Again, you could have two people experience the same event, but one walks away framing their life as being "ruined", while the other does not. Even if you don't subscribe to the idea that each moment is its own life, you can still see each moment as a chance to start over.

How the "Ruined Life" Belief Kills Motivation

Another side effect of framing our entire life in such dramatic terms is that it can undermine our motivation. If we believe life can never be made "untarnished" again, we may lose the drive to pursue new opportunities or engage with our interests. We might end up spending the rest of our existence mourning what we see as a tainted life. This demotivating effect is more common in those who believe they have only one life.

By contrast, someone who sees each point in time as its own self-contained life is unlikely to have their motivation affected in the same way. They view many of their future lives as "unruined" by the event. Because they don't believe their life as a whole has been spoiled, they aren't stuck mourning it for the rest of their days.

This shows that it's not the undesirable event itself that demotivates us, but how we frame its impact on our life. Ironically, what's more likely to "ruin" our lives going forward is the belief that they've already been ruined. To avoid this demotivating effect, we need to stop framing life in these terms.

THE THREE MOST COMMON QUESTIONS ABOUT LIFE

When we talk about life, three questions tend to come up again and again:

- What is the *meaning* of life?
- What is the *purpose* of life?
- What is the *point* of life?

As with any question we try to answer, we can only arrive at what we honestly believe is logically consistent with our observed experiences. We can't rule out the possibility that something we haven't yet observed could contradict our conclusion. So while we may genuinely believe our answer is true, we can never prove it with 100% certainty. In the case of these specific questions about life, this means we can only honestly believe — but never prove — that we've found its true meaning, purpose, or point.

We may have been conditioned to accept only answers we can prove with 100% certainty. Because of this, we might even reject ideas we honestly believe are logically consistent with our observed experiences. To begin accepting such answers at all, we need to challenge the belief that only what can be proven with absolute certainty is worth trusting.

We'll now explore what I honestly believe are the answers to these three questions, based on my experiences to date.

What Is the Meaning of Life?

Before we can understand what the meaning of life is, we need to first be clear on what "meaning" itself is. What are we trying to do when looking for the meaning of something *generally*? For example, what are we trying to do when looking for the meaning behind a particular painting?

We come to understand what "meaning" is by considering what we generate it in response to. We produce meaning in response to the experiences we observe. When we have a sensorial or emotional experience and form a thought to explain it, we are generating meaning. For instance, when we look at a painting and interpret it, that interpretation becomes the painting's meaning to us. In other words, the *explanation within the thought* is the meaning we assign to the experience. Put simply: whenever we think about something, we are generating its meaning. There is no distinction between thinking and generating meaning. They are one and the same.

The particular meaning a person assigns to an experience is shaped by what they honestly believe to be logically consistent with their observed experiences so far. These beliefs, in turn, are influenced by the biological and environmental factors that have shaped them. The biological factors relate to the physical structure of their brain, while the environmental factors include what they were taught growing up and the experiences they've accumulated. As a result, two people observing the same painting may arrive at similar or different meanings, depending on the similarities and differences in their biological makeup and life experiences.

Because we are always thinking, we are always generating meaning. For those concerned about not generating meaning at all, there's no need to worry. It's virtually impossible to stop. Our minds produce meaning constantly and abundantly. What we should be more concerned about is whether the meaning we consciously generate aligns with what we honestly believe deep down, or whether it's a form of self-deception. If we sense an internal contradiction in the meaning we've assigned to an experience, we might deceive ourselves into ignoring it. With enough mental fortitude, we can face that contradiction and adjust our understanding. Without it, we're likely to deny the inconsistency, and hold onto a meaning we no longer sincerely believe.

Now that we're clear on what "meaning" is — an explanation of an experience contained in a thought — we can begin to understand what the meaning of life is. According to my basic definition, "life is the sensorial, emotional, and conceptual experience of biologically existing in each moment". So, the meaning of life is simply the thoughts we generate in response to these experiences. If we see ourselves as having only one life, then its meaning comes from everything we've experienced. It's the accumulation of all the thinking we've done in response to all our moments.

If instead we see each moment as its own complete life, then the meaning of that life comes from what we're thinking in that instant. It's the meaning we generate in response to the experiences happening right then. It is the meaning of *that* life at that point in time. Each of these lives will have a meaning that is utterly unique. No two lives will share the exact same meaning, because each moment contains a one-of-a-kind mix of sensations, emotions, and thoughts. And since that combination never repeats itself exactly, neither will the meaning we assign to it.

Most people believe the answer to the question "what is the meaning of life?" lies in just one thing. They assume that only experiences related to that one domain give life meaning, implying that everything else lacks significance. But I think anyone who believes this hasn't clearly grasped what "meaning" itself is generally. If they had, they would recognize that meaning is generated in every experience. They would see how reductive it is to claim that the meaning of life revolves around only one thing.

When we believe that life's meaning comes from only one thing, it can dull the satisfaction we feel from anything outside that narrow focus. If we don't see an activity as meaningful, we're less open to it. We're more likely to disengage or dismiss it entirely. But if we instead recognize that we generate meaning in every single moment, then almost every experience can feel meaningful in some way. This shift makes us receptive to a wider range of activities. And when we also see the meaning generated in each moment as entirely unique, we become more attentive and curious. We become more willing to explore the distinctive value each moment holds.

What Is the Purpose of Life?

Before we can understand what the purpose of life is, we first need to be clear on what it means to have a "purpose" in *general*. To me, it's quite simple: having a purpose is the same as having an intention. As long as we have one, we have the other.

In each moment, our minds are generating intentions, whether consciously or subconsciously. If we see purpose as the same thing as intention, then we can say we have two types of purpose in every moment. First, there's our *general purpose*: to optimize our well-being. Then, there's our *specific purpose*: the particular physical or mental pursuit we intend to carry out in that moment to serve our general aim. While our general purpose stays constant from moment to moment, our specific purpose can shift. This is because the forms of gratification we seek may change, which in turn alters the actions we're inclined to take.

Since we always have both general and specific purposes at any given time, it means we always have a purpose of some kind. We are never without one. Even if we haven't consciously identified our specific purpose in a given moment, we still have the underlying general purpose of optimizing our enjoyment.

So, what is the purpose of life? What is the purpose of a living being experiencing what we call "life"? That depends on whether we're referring to life's general purpose or its specific purpose. In my view, the general purpose is to optimize satisfaction. And through that, enhance the experience of life itself. As mentioned, while this broader aim remains constant, our specific purpose shifts as the forms of enjoyment we seek change from moment to moment. At one point, life's specific purpose might be to engage in a particular activity; at another, it may become something else entirely.

Where do these purposes come from? Both our general and specific purposes only come into existence at the moment they are generated by the brain. The general purpose is one that happens to be constantly generated. Given how universal this aim is among humans — and how persistent it remains throughout our lives — I believe it arises purely from the physical structure of our brains. It appears to be largely unaffected by the environment we grow up in. In contrast, our specific purpose at any given moment is shaped by a mix of biological and environmental factors. The similarities or differences between the specific purposes of two individuals will depend on the similarities or differences in both their biology and life experiences.

Is there another purpose designated to us before birth that we are supposed to fulfill? Personally, I haven't seen any compelling evidence that would lead me to believe so. I'm open to the possibility that such a purpose exists, but I can't act on it until more convincing information is available. I won't outright deny its existence, but for now, I'll live as though it doesn't. The purposes I focus on are the general and specific ones that arise in my mind from moment to moment. These are the purposes I aim to discover and explore.

What often makes it hard for people to let go of the idea of a designated purpose is the belief that their happiness depends on fulfilling it. Once we stop holding that belief, it becomes easier to let go of the search.

Believing that the only purpose that matters is one set before birth can lead us to dismiss the general and specific purposes that arise within us moment to moment. When we don't engage with these purposes and the activities that flow from them, this can reduce the contentment we would otherwise be getting. Maybe we don't even bother with these undertakings. We could be missing out on all this enjoyment to pursue something that does not exist.

What Is the Point of Life?

When we ask what the point of life is, we're usually trying to understand what *desirable outcomes* might come from our existence as a whole.

To me, this isn't the kind of point we should be looking for. Instead, we should focus on the desirable outcomes that can be attained *within each moment of our existence*. In each moment, the point is to optimize our well-being. This ongoing aim motivates us to engage in physical and mental pursuits that bring about the specific forms of enjoyment we're seeking. We are never without this point.

Some people argue that life has no point. But in my view, these arguments often rely on assumptions that can be easily challenged. Let's now take a closer look at some of the most common ones.

The first argument is that "we will eventually be forgotten". It would indeed be pointless if the *only* reason to do anything is to be remembered. But I don't act for the sake of being remembered. I act because of the point that arises in each instant. There is still something to enjoy right now. Whether I am remembered later is irrelevant to me.

The second argument is that "we are going to die anyway". It would indeed seem pointless if the *sole* reason to do anything were to completely prevent death. But again, I do things because of the point that arises in each moment. That's not to say I'm entirely unconcerned about death. I don't want to die, and I'll act to prevent it when I can. Still, recognizing that I will die in the future doesn't nullify the point that exists in the present. Again, there is still a moment to be enjoyed.

The third argument is that "nothing matters". When people say this, they usually mean that "nothing matters to the universe". But I don't see how anyone could realistically claim to understand the universe well enough to determine what does or doesn't matter to it. And even if we could, why should that matter to us? What's important is what matters from our individual vantage points. We should be indifferent to whether the universe "cares" or not. What it "thinks" is irrelevant. In my view, each moment matters to us and is important because it affects our satisfaction.

The above arguments suggesting that life has no point are too focused on whether the moment we're experiencing right now will matter in the long run. But it doesn't need to matter in the long run. It just needs to matter now.

THE FUNDAMENTAL NARRATIVE WE FIND OURSELVES IN

In response to the experience of life, we can't help but form a narrative about ourselves. This narrative is "our story". One of our goals, I believe, is to become aware of the *fundamental narrative* we're living. The one that has shaped our existence all along, even if we haven't yet found the words to articulate it.

In my view, this fundamental narrative is about our progression through the three core roles we occupy in life:

- The "scientist" who seeks to understand their experiences.
- The "warrior" who faces challenges.
- The "craftsman" who puts together creative experiences.

At any given moment, we tend to occupy all three roles *simultaneously*. However, the *extent* to which we inhabit each one can vary from one moment to the next. We remain in these roles for nearly the entirety of our lives, as they are intrinsic to the human experience.

This narrative can be broken down into two arcs: a primary one and a secondary one.

The Primary Arc of This Fundamental Narrative

The primary arc can be loosely divided into three acts.

Act 1 is where we recognize that our *fundamental want* is to optimize satisfaction. This same desire drives the behavior of the three core roles we occupy. It is the pursuit of well-being that motivates the scientist to understand experience, the warrior to face challenges, and the craftsman to create.

Act 2 is when we come to realize that our emotional enjoyment and distress arise primarily from the *internal* mental frameworks we've adopted — not from the attainment of *external* things. We recognize that, as children, we found happiness through a mind that was open and engaged with the present. We now see that this openness has been disrupted by the mental frameworks we've developed over time.

This realization shifts how each of the three core roles behaves:

- The scientist now seeks to better understand and map what is happening within their own mind, rather than just what is happening in the external world. They shift the

focus of learning inward, paying more attention to internal
patterns than external ones.

- The warrior now looks to confront internal challenges
  more than external ones. This is a warrior who recognizes
  that genuine peace comes from mastering oneself. The
  dragon every warrior must ultimately face and overcome
  is the one within.
- The craftsman now aims to represent what's happening
  inside the mind rather than what's happening in the
  external world.

All three core roles have now "turned the eye inward", recognizing how essential self-examination is to optimizing well-being.

Act 3 is where we remove the disruption caused to our playful
mind by our mental frameworks. This involves us:

- Dismantling the mental frameworks that block our
  satisfaction and cause us pain.
- Completing enough of our model of reality.

Each of the core roles performs a specific function in Act 3:

- The scientist understands the mental frameworks that
  interfere with the playful mind and how to dismantle
  them. They also develop a model of reality that feels
  complete enough to live by.
- The warrior builds the mental fortitude and courage to
  confront the frameworks that cause emotional hurt.
- The craftsman assembles creative experiences as a way of
  exploring mental frameworks that cause pain. For
  example, they might construct works of fiction in which
  characters wrestle with these frameworks. The craftsman
  also uses creative expression to explore their evolving
  picture of reality.

By the end of the primary arc, we have cleared away the major sources of disruption to the playful mind and our experience of happiness. Chapters 1–10 have been dedicated to completing this arc.

The Secondary Arc of This Fundamental Narrative

The secondary arc is about using our liberated playful mind to engage with our experiences and discover different satisfying emotions to combine with happiness.

At times, we're deliberate about the specific emotion we want to use to enhance our happiness. To bring it out, we identify the types of actions that tend to trigger that emotion. How we uncover the actions that evoke the most fundamental of these feelings will be explored in Chapter 11.

Other times, we're not so picky about which emotion we want to generate. We're content with whatever satisfying feelings arise from fully engaging in whatever we're doing. Since we're not seeking anything specific, we don't actively try to enhance our happiness by chasing particular emotions or actions. We're simply happy to explore and try things out.

During the secondary arc, the three core roles evolve to take on new functions:

- The scientist now seeks to learn how to trigger specific enjoyable feelings to enhance happiness.
- The warrior now looks to stay vigilant against re-adopting mental frameworks that cause pain. If such frameworks return, the warrior must rely on their mental fortitude and courage to undo them once more.
- The craftsman now aims to assemble creative experiences that trigger specific enjoyable emotions, leveraging whatever insight the scientist has gained.

I don't see this secondary arc as needing to be broken down into acts like the primary arc. To summarize, it's really about learning how to trigger specific satisfying emotions, and then acting on that insight.

Combining the Primary Arc and the Secondary Arc Together

When we look at the primary and secondary arcs together, we can see the fundamental narrative as a whole: the saga of optimizing satisfaction through self-actualization.

"Self-actualization" can mean different things to different people. To me, it means understanding how to make ourselves happy. The primary arc is about identifying the mental frameworks that interfere with our happiness and removing them. The secondary arc is about learning how to enhance that happiness by bringing in other satisfying emotions and then acting on that insight.

In this saga of optimizing satisfaction through self-actualization, there is an even more fundamental role that we occupy at all times: *the experiencer*. Within each moment, the experiencer has sensations, emotions, and thoughts, and it is through these that they experience both satisfaction and suffering. The experiencer harnesses the *collective attributes* of the scientist, warrior, and craftsman to optimize their satisfaction, and thereby, optimize the experience of life. First, the experiencer has to stop interfering with their own happiness; then they learn how to deliberately enhance it. Since this saga is about the experiencer, I also refer to it as the "saga of the human experience".

The Benefits of Recognizing the Fundamental Narrative We Are In

By seeing the fundamental narrative, we have a greater sense of orientation. We can place ourselves somewhere along this narrative and see where we are headed. Without identifying this fundamental story, it is easy to feel disorientated.

Recognizing the fundamental narrative as a journey into ourselves can give us a sense of adventure. At the beginning, we learn how to navigate and explore the mind safely. While initially difficult, at some point we learn to enjoy the experience of such an exploration. This is an adventure we experience moment by moment — through sensations, feelings, and thoughts. It never ends while we are alive, for there are always new interactions with reality to explore and discover. There are always more combinations of enjoyable emotions to find. The journey continues, even when we've already found a foundational happiness.

8

―――――

IMPROVING HOW
WE FEEL ABOUT LIFE

When we were younger, it was easier to reflect on life and generate more satisfying feelings toward it. But as we grew older, we adopted mental frameworks that began to block those emotions. In this chapter, we'll explore how to dismantle those thought patterns and, as much as possible, restore the ease with which we once experienced these feelings. Our goal is to reclaim the following:

- Excitement
- Wonder
- Appreciation
- Fulfillment
- Optimism

RESTORING EXCITEMENT

If we want to feel excited about life, we have to feel excited about the activities that make it up. Why did our activities energize us so much when we were younger? Where does this feeling come from?

We feel excited about something when we see it as *different* from what we've done before. As children, we more often encountered new and unfamiliar experiences, making it easier to feel energized by what we were doing. As we got older, genuinely new pursuits became harder to find. As a result, so did that same sense of excitement.

Being Excited Over Radical Differences vs. Subtle Differences

The main problem is that we're accustomed to looking only for *radical* differences in the things we do, not the *subtle* ones. When something doesn't seem drastically different, we often assume it's no different at all from what we've done before. As a result, we feel no excitement and start to believe that life no longer offers any new experiences. What we often overlook is that these experiences still contain many subtle distinctions.

When we train ourselves to notice these nuances, it becomes easier to feel excited. Two people can do the same activity, but the one who notices the subtle differences is likely to enjoy it more. While this kind of excitement may not be as intense as the kind sparked by radical distinctions, it isn't inherently lesser. At its core, it's still a form of excitement that can be quite satisfying.

What makes a pursuit "radically" different as opposed to "subtly" different? I consider a pursuit radically different when the combination of sensations, emotions, and thoughts it produces is strikingly distinct from what I've previously experienced. In contrast, I see it as subtly different when the variation is more nuanced, when the distinctions are there but not immediately obvious or intense.

Take music, for example. Listening to jazz for the first time after a lifetime of only hearing pop is a radical difference because the rhythm, instruments, and structure are strikingly unfamiliar. Hearing two jazz songs from different eras might offer a subtle difference, such as one feeling smoother and the other more experimental. Even when the same jazz song is played live twice, there can be *finer distinctions* in how the musician holds a note slightly longer or brings a different energy to the performance.

While it may become harder with age to find pursuits that are dramatically distinct, we can always find ones that are at least finely varied in their mix of sensations, emotions, and thoughts. No activity is ever exactly the same as another. With this mindset, I believe we can carry a sense of excitement into almost everything we do, and by extension, toward life itself. We begin to see life as still offering new, if subtle, experiences.

Part of the reason I find subtle distinctions exciting is that the ability to notice them feels like a genuine privilege. When we were younger, our pursuits were often both radically and subtly different, but we were so preoccupied with the radical aspects that we over-looked the subtle ones. At the time, it was hard for us to notice and develop an appreciation for these finer distinctions.

As we grow older and become more familiar with radical differ-ences, we become better at noticing subtle ones. When we begin to see these subtle distinctions, we find ourselves experiencing some-thing very *nuanced*. These are nuances in the blend of sensations, feelings, and thoughts in each moment of doing the thing.

Let's use riding a bike as an example. As children, the experience felt radically new. The thrill of balance, speed, and movement was overwhelming and exciting. But as adults, once the novelty has worn off, we start to notice more delicate differences: the quiet resistance of the wind, the subtle shift in terrain beneath the tires, how our posture affects the ride, or the way our mind feels differently depending on the route or time of day. These subtleties were always there. We just weren't attuned to them yet.

Such experiential mixes are utterly unique and never to be repeated in exactly the same way. That's pretty exciting, I think. I feel privileged to be able to notice something so precise, to have devel-oped an eye for detail that is sensorial, emotional, and conceptual. It's part of why I feel somewhat privileged to be an adult. It's not a "bet-ter" experience than being a child, just a different one. Adulthood brings its own forms of interest and excitement.

I don't think it's impossible to find pursuits that are radically different as we get older. We should never rule it out. Many times, I've assumed an activity would feel only subtly different from what I'd already done, only to discover that it brought sensations, emotions, and thoughts that were drastically distinct. I mention this because I think many of us make the same assumption and, as a result, choose not to even give some things a try. In doing so, we may miss out on experiences that we would have discovered to be radically different — if only we had taken that first step.

Increasing Excitement Toward Sensations and Feelings, Not Just Concepts

Another reason we may struggle to feel excited about many things is that we've been conditioned to value concepts over sensations and feelings.

Because of this conditioning, we tend to only get excited about things that offer new concepts. Our ability to feel excited by different sensations and emotions has been muted. When we were younger, we hadn't yet been conditioned in this way, which allowed us to feel excitement toward a much broader range of pursuits. We enjoyed experiences not just for the concepts they introduced, but for the variety of sensations and feelings they evoked.

This conditioning to value only concepts likely influenced the kinds of interests we pursued over time. As a result, we became more inclined to select activities we believed would expose us to new ideas, while overlooking — or even dismissing — those that offered primarily different sensations and feelings.

We should work to remove this conditioning that leads us to value only concepts, so we can more easily feel excited about pursuits that offer rich sensorial and emotional experiences. I believe those who focus solely on the conceptual will eventually feel that something essential is missing from their experience of life.

We can begin to remove this conditioning by recognizing that sensations and feelings are at least as important as concepts, if not more so. Their importance becomes clear when we reflect on what we fundamentally want: to optimize our well-being. And well-being is defined in their terms. At our core, we want to increase our sensorial and emotional enjoyment and minimize our sensorial and emotional pain.

Our fundamental wants are not in terms of concepts. As discussed in Chapter 5, concepts are tools which help us obtain what we primarily desire. They allow us to understand causal relationships in reality, which we can then leverage to attain the sensations and emotions we seek. In this sense, concepts are a means to an end. They are not themselves an end. In other words, concepts are not inherently important for their own sake. They actually *derive their importance* from what they help us attain. Concepts matter because the sensations and feelings they help us reach matter.

RESTORING WONDER

We tend to feel a sense of wonder towards experiences we don't comprehend very well. But once we believe we grasp an experience well enough, the wonder we produce towards it is much less.

When we were children, we didn't understand much of what we experienced. Because so little was familiar, we felt wonder toward almost everything — including the experience of life itself. All of reality felt like a magic trick, the secrets of which were still hidden from us. But as we grew older and began to understand more, fewer experiences inspired that same sense of wonder. We had learned too much about how the trick worked. As time passed, our sense of wonder toward life became less and less.

How do we restore our sense of wonder toward life? One way is to look at every experience and find a *shared fundamental aspect* we will likely never fully understand. This quality runs through all our experiences and will probably always remain at least somewhat incomprehensible. Realizing this can help rekindle our sense of wonder, both toward what we observe in any given moment and toward life as a whole. It's the recognition that something essential about this "magic trick" remains beyond our grasp, and likely always will.

When I look at my experiences, I notice two fundamental aspects that are present in all of them. And both, I would argue, are somewhat incomprehensible.

How the Universe Came into Existence

Everything we experience has taken place within the universe. But how did the universe itself come into being? There are two common theories, yet both seem incomprehensible to me on some level.

One theory is that a sentient entity physically created the universe. But the very existence of such an entity is itself somewhat incomprehensible, both in terms of how it functions and how it came into being.

Another theory is that the universe was not brought into existence. It just simply exists. Its existence has no prior cause. While this idea is understandable on some level, it is also incomprehensible on another, as our human minds are accustomed to seeing everything as having a cause.

How the Brain Creates the Experience of Life in Our Minds

This is to do with how our brains generate the sensorial, emotional, and conceptual experiences we observe. While we may grasp to *some* degree that our brains create this experience through processing specific electrical signals, we will never comprehend the *deepest depths* of how this works. We will never have all the details.

In my view, the creation of the universe and the creation of experience in the mind are two of the greatest magic tricks we will ever encounter. They are also tricks that we will never fully understand the deepest secrets of.

RESTORING APPRECIATION AND GRATITUDE

Many of life's complaints stem from not getting what we want. But even when we do get what we want, we may not feel especially appreciative or grateful. Why is that?

When we were younger, it was easier to feel this way. But as we got older, those feelings were often blocked when we received something we had developed an *egotistical sense of entitlement* toward. The satisfaction was diminished because we saw it as something *owed* to us. In our minds, we were simply receiving what had rightfully been ours all along.

On what basis do we egotistically believe that something is owed to us? It depends on the person. Sometimes, we think it's owed simply by virtue of existing, as if being born entitles us to specific things. Other times, we believe we deserve it because we've worked for it and put in the effort.

On the other hand, a person without a sense of entitlement doesn't believe something is owed to them. They don't assume that simply by existing, they deserve it. Nor do they believe it's owed just because they've worked hard or put in the effort. If they do receive it, they're more likely to see themselves as *lucky*. Recognizing how fortunate we are to have something is essential to feeling genuine appreciation and gratitude for it.

If we struggle to feel this way, it may be because an egotistic sense of entitlement is getting in the way. When we believe we're entitled to *everything we receive*, we limit our ability to feel satisfied with all of it. To restore these satisfying emotions, we need to break the ego's belief that we are owed everything.

The notion that we're entitled to everything begins to unravel when we ask ourselves *who*, exactly, we believe owes us these things. More often than not, we're speaking vaguely about the "universe". The universe does not owe us anything, and simply saying so does not make it true. It's as if we're trying to impose obligations on the universe to give us what we want. These are obligations it never agreed to in the first place. It's a bit presumptuous to believe it owes us anything. Since there's no cosmic obligation toward us, I think we're lucky to get anything at all. So even when I work toward a goal and don't get the outcome I hoped for, I still feel lucky for all the interesting experiences I gained along the way — and for everything I already have.

Recognizing that this sense of entitlement comes from the ego may encourage us to put more effort into letting it go. After all, most of us don't like to think of ourselves as being controlled by our ego in any way.

FIND GREATER FULFILLMENT BY CHALLENGING THE EGO

To feel fulfilled in life, we need to generate that feeling through our pursuits. However, various mental frameworks can block fulfillment in activities that would otherwise produce it. In this section, we'll explore how the ego gets in the way and how to remove the disruption.

As we saw in Chapter 1, the ego's fear of looking foolish for sincerely enjoying an activity can interfere with that enjoyment. That same fear can also diminish our sense of fulfillment. To prevent the ego from limiting this feeling, we need to help it let go of concerns about how we're perceived. This involves examining the reasons someone else might view the activity as foolish to find fulfilling. And strongly questioning whether those reasons should matter to us or to our ego at all.

The Pursuit Is Foolish if It Doesn't Provide an Important Enough Challenge

One reason a pursuit may be seen as foolish is that it is not regarded as posing an *important enough* challenge to warrant being fulfilled by it. But that's not for others to decide. Only the individual can determine which challenges matter to them. What others think is irrelevant. I consider any challenge I choose to take on as important, even if others see it differently.

I also tend not to view the challenges I face as more or less important than one another. While it is sometimes possible to classify them in this way, I generally see my obstacles as being equally important for *different* reasons. This is regardless of the "size" of the obstacle. I don't necessarily see "big" challenges as more important than "small" ones. They can be important in various ways, each satisfying unique needs or desires. They scratch different itches. As a result, challenges can offer various forms of fulfillment. These are simply variations of the same core emotion, none inherently better or worse than the others. They provide roughly equal levels of satisfaction, just in their own ways.

We might also assume that a challenge can only be important if it is serious. No, the obstacle doesn't have to be serious and dour for it to matter to us. It can be important while being fun at the same time.

The Pursuit Is Foolish if We Aren't Successful While Doing It

Some people may see it as foolish to find something emotionally rewarding if we aren't "successful" in doing it. Success is often defined as attaining a particular final outcome that is desirable. Those who operate under such a definition will permit themselves to feel emotionally rewarded and fulfilled *only* upon reaching the final outcome — not during the moments that lead to it.

The way I see it, there are challenges at every step of the way while doing most things. As a result, I am able to feel emotionally rewarded and fulfilled *in every moment* leading to the final result. Fulfillment isn't just found at the end, but throughout. This steady emotional uplift helps us keep going when the activity gets tough.

To be clear: being emotionally rewarded and fulfilled stems less from overcoming each obstacle and more from *rising to meet them.* Such contentment comes primarily from *sincerely trying* to face these challenges, even though there is no guarantee they will be surmounted. In this way, this is another type of "success" that can be had in *each moment of doing an activity.* There are opportunities for such success throughout the course of the task and not just when we get to the end of it. There is more than one type of success that is worth pursuing.

That being said, I find it far more important to succeed in this way of each moment of the task than in the more conventional sense of reaching a specific final outcome. I see getting this final outcome as a nice-to-have rather than an essential part of the pursuit. Even if I succeed in the conventional sense — by attaining the intended result — what really makes the activity emotionally rewarding is rising to the challenges along the way.

I think the reason I don't feel as emotionally rewarded or fulfilled by reaching the final desired result is that I see its attainment as a mix of skill and luck. My skill can increase the odds of meeting this objective, but I can only do so much. There are all these other factors that still remain largely out of my control. So when I do get the result I want, I tend to attribute that success to luck more than my skill.

It's still satisfying to get what I desired at the end, but primarily because I appreciate how lucky I am to be getting it. To the extent that I find conventional success to be satisfying, I enjoy it mostly on this level. I think the reason we place so much emphasis on reaching the final outcome — while often overlooking the moments leading up to it — is that we've been conditioned to believe the ending matters most. But every moment matters to us because each one affects our satisfaction.

Pursuing Success Without Ego

If you see "success" only as reaching the final desired outcome, I suggest pursuing that goal without letting your ego worry about looking foolish if you fall short. When the ego fixates on this fear, it can stop you from attempting things where conventional success isn't guaranteed. You may also avoid brand new pursuits where you have little or no experience, or more challenging versions of activities you're already familiar with. You may miss out on:

- Acquiring new skills or maturing existing ones.
- Having experiences that can be fun, interesting, and engaging.
- Having experiences that pose a different set of challenges to what you're used to. As a result, you miss out on the

different ways you can be emotionally rewarded and
fulfilled.

All of the above can be gained simply by *attempting* the endeavor.
Even without reaching the desired end result, you still experience
and learn so much just by sincerely giving it a go. And these aren't
rewards reserved only for the end. They can be found in each
moment of the process. There's enjoyment, challenge, and engagement to be had all throughout. That's why what I usually look
forward to isn't the final outcome, but what unfolds along the way. To
miss out on all of this because your ego is nervous about seeming
foolish for not reaching conventional success. That, in my view, is the
greater foolishness.

Broadly speaking, we should not let our ego be the primary motivator behind our desire for success. When it is, we chase achievement
mainly to "prove" something to someone, hoping it says something
impressive about us in the eyes of others. We want people to see us in
a particular way, to assign the label of "success" to who we are as a
person. But this is not an emotionally healthy reason to pursue goals.
It nurtures the insecure part of us that desires external validation.
Even when we succeed, the underlying insecurity remains unresolved. Just because we've achieved something this time doesn't mean
we'll do so again. Any success that we have while still being hostage
to this insecurity will not be that satisfying.

The way to stop our ego from being the primary motivator behind
our ambitions is to assert that we don't need to prove anything to
anybody. We don't need others to label us as a "success", nor are we
emotionally affected if they don't. When we adopt this mindset, we
can still pursue success, but not out of insecurity or a need for validation. We're not trying to boost our self-esteem or think more highly of
ourselves. We're simply drawn to the experience itself because we
believe it will be interesting and enjoyable.

With the ego no longer in control, we're freer to choose pursuits
not based on our chances of success, but on whether they offer experiences we find interesting, fun, and engaging. Another benefit of

letting go of ego as the primary driver is that we no longer feel embarrassed or ashamed if we don't succeed. This is because those feelings stem from the ego in the first place.

FIND GREATER FULFILLMENT BY NOT EXPECTING SO MUCH OF IT

We may have been conditioned to expect that life will offer experiences that bring a deep sense of reward. When we hold this expectation, we tend to compare what we're actually feeling with what we had hoped to experience. If that comparison shows a shortfall, it can lead to a feeling of being unfulfilled — and even despair. We might be engaged in activities that are genuinely rewarding, but because we expected more, a feeling of discontent still arises. In general, the higher our expectations, the more likely we are to feel unfulfilled.

In my view, this response arises only because we're comparing what we received with what we anticipated. Without that contrast, the feeling wouldn't arise at all. We can avoid this discontent by letting go of expectations about how fulfilling our pursuits should be. This frees us to appreciate whatever genuine reward we do experience, without smothering it under assumptions of what it *should* have been. Doing something that brings little or no fulfillment doesn't automatically make us feel unfulfilled. That reaction only surfaces when we expected more than we received.

More Specific Expectations We Should Let Go Of

Many of us have been conditioned to expect that we'll one day find something that delivers a *mythological* level of fulfillment. What we expect is so immense that it moves beyond what is likely in reality and into the realm of fantasy. Believing we can find something that produces this kind of emotional reward is like searching for unicorns or chasing Bigfoot. While the fulfillment we get from our pursuits can vary, few experiences, if any, reach these imagined heights. If we continue to expect something that delivers that much, we all but guarantee a sense of disappointment. We might gain a great deal of genuine fulfillment from an activity, yet still feel unfulfilled afterward, simply because it didn't measure up to what we imagined.

We may have also been conditioned to expect to find a pursuit that produces fulfillment for a *mythological duration*. With this expectation, we hope to discover something that leaves us feeling rewarded long after the activity is over. Perhaps even for the rest of our lives. But again, this is like chasing a unicorn or pursuing Bigfoot. The emotional rewards can vary from one activity to another, but few, if any, produce something that endures for such an imagined length of time.

Once again, we may feel discontent — even after a rewarding experience — because we've compared what we received with what we expected. We can avoid this by not making the comparison in the first place. And the most effective way to do that is to let go of any expectations about how long the feeling should last. When we stop making that demand, we no longer feel disappointed just because the sense of reward was brief. Personally, when I feel fulfilled, I place no demands on its duration. I simply enjoy it for however long it's there.

If we're going to form any expectations about how long this emotion can last for an undertaking, we should focus only on being fulfilled in our *moments*, rather than for the rest of our lives. Think not about what makes life fulfilling, but what makes each moment so.

We may have adopted the belief that we can't be happy unless we find fulfillment that matches the size and duration of what we expected. This is a happiness conditional statement. Its impact is two-fold. First, when we don't receive the emotion we anticipated, we may feel despair on top of feeling unfulfilled. Second, believing our happiness depends on finding large and long-lasting fulfillment makes it hard to let go of that expectation. It's difficult to release something we think our happiness relies on. But when we break down this conditional belief and accept that we can be happy without that kind of fulfillment, the despair fades, and we can finally let go of the expectation.

Seeing Fulfillment as a Bonus, Not a Need

After thinking through all of this, I've come to see fulfillment as a *nice-to-have* emotion rather than an essential one. My happiness comes from having a playful mind; it doesn't depend on finding pursuits that feel deeply fulfilling. I can also enhance this happiness with other emotions like excitement, fun, or peace. In doing so, I can create emotional combinations that feel satisfying without needing fulfillment to be part of the mix. I don't need that emotion to be happy.

When I engage in an activity, my main aim is to be involved in a way that makes the experience satisfying on some level. From moment to moment, I focus on being content and happy, not on chasing some deeper emotional payoff. If the experience doesn't feel especially fulfilling, that's fine. It doesn't leave me feeling deprived. And if that deeper sense of reward does happen to arise, I simply treat it as a bonus.

FIND GREATER FULFILLMENT BY NOT RULING IT OUT PREMATURELY

While the previous section focused on not overestimating how fulfilling a new activity might be, this one is about not assuming it won't be fulfilling at all. After all, if we make that assumption, we might be discouraged from trying it in the first place. It could actually turn out to be deeply rewarding — but we never discover that because we don't give it a try. On what basis do we make these assumptions without firsthand experience?

Often, we base them on our observations of other people doing it. For example, we might watch a theater actor on stage and assume, based on what we see, that the being a performer wouldn't feel emotionally rewarding. But in that moment, we're trying to imagine what the experience of being that performer is like. How *reliable* is that imagination from the standpoint of a viewer who's never done it before? After all, all we have to go on are the sensations, emotions, and thoughts we experience while watching. What we imagine from the outside can differ greatly from the actual inner experience of the person doing the activity.

We also make assumptions about what new activities will be like based on past experiences with things that appear similar. Continuing with the same example, suppose we once acted in a TV show and didn't find it emotionally rewarding. Because we see TV and theater acting as closely related, we might assume that performing on stage would also leave us unfulfilled.

That being said, even if a new activity resembles something we've done before, it can still turn out to be a very different experience in a major way. Sure, the fundamentals of screen and theater acting may be similar, but the details can differ significantly. Both involve acting, but only one involves performing live in front of the general public. The sensations, emotions, and thoughts of someone acting for a film crew can feel entirely different from those of someone performing on stage before a live audience. So even when we draw on past experiences, our assumptions about a new undertaking can still be unreliable.

Is there a reliable way to tell whether something new will be emotionally rewarding without trying it? In my view, the answer is no. The best way to find out is to give the activity a sincere try and pay attention to how we feel while doing it. We only *discover* that we enjoy a pursuit when we actually start doing it. We might find it's more fun, interesting, or engaging than we expected, even if it doesn't turn out to be deeply fulfilling. It could still be satisfying in its own way.

This is why I think, generally speaking, we should try just about everything once. We might be surprised at what we end up liking. By avoiding something simply because we assume it won't be rewarding, we risk missing out on experiences that are gratifying in other forms.

Don't Rule Out Fulfillment in Things We're Not Passionate About

Many of us have been conditioned to think that we should only pursue what we're passionate about, as only those pursuits will lead to emotional rewards. So when it comes to things we're not passionate about, we tend to rule out the possibility that they could be fulfilling. As a result, we either don't attempt them at all, or we do them without fully engaging.

For me, I would struggle to identify something I'm genuinely passionate about. There are things I enjoy tremendously and find rewarding — like learning to play the piano — but I wouldn't say I'm passionate about them. Even writing, which I find fulfilling, isn't something I'd describe with that word. The issue isn't that the activities themselves are terrible. It's that "passion" feels like such a high bar that it doesn't feel appropriate to apply to anything. At least not for me. And I suspect only a relative handful of people genuinely feel passionate about something. Musician, actors, and athletes come to mind.

My point is that if we happen to be someone who hasn't found a strong personal calling — or simply doesn't feel that kind of intense enthusiasm — it doesn't stop us from discovering things that are enjoyable and deeply fulfilling. Even in my day job as a business analyst, I wouldn't say I have a burning passion for it, but I get a lot of fun and fulfillment from the problem-solving aspect. Every day, I'm presented with a new puzzle to figure out.

FIND GREATER FULFILLMENT BY LOOKING BEYOND NOVELTY

When choosing which activities to pursue, many of us use a key criterion: it must appear radically different from what we've done before. In practice, this means we gravitate only toward experiences that seem dramatically new and overlook those that are merely subtly different. It also means we often stop doing something once we've moved past the initial stages.

At first, the activity may feel exciting precisely because it's unfamiliar. But as we grow more accustomed to it, the sense of novelty fades. The experiences it offers — the sensations, feelings, and thoughts — start to feel less distinct. At that point, we may see it as offering only minor variations, and our interest begins to wane, prompting us to search for the next radically different pursuit. I believe this is why many people are enthusiastic when they begin learning a musical instrument, only to give it up shortly after.

How This Desire for Novelty Impacts Our Levels of Fulfillment

When we're starting something new, we experience a particular kind of fulfillment, one that comes from rising to challenges while our skillset is still developing. However, if we *only* do things in their early stages — and don't go beyond — we miss out on other emotional rewards. Two in particular come to mind.

The first is the fulfillment that comes with rising to meet obstacles that are difficult, even when one has developed a *high* level of skill. Beyond the early stages of an activity, there are still new challenges to face. Even with moderate or advanced ability, there are always ways to push that skill further and continue developing. While we may be a master in some respects, we remain a novice in others. I would think that many experienced musicians feel the same way. From this perspective, even in the later stages of a pursuit, there's still ample opportunity for fulfillment, while continuing to find it fun, interesting, and engaging.

The second type of fulfillment we miss out on by prioritizing novelty is the kind that comes from building a deep, long-term relationship with an undertaking. When we've developed such a relationship, it feels as though we've gone on a journey with it. That journey may begin with the excitement of how radically different it seems. But over time, it matures into a fascination with the nuanced sensations, emotions, and thoughts that unfold in each moment. An endeavor that becomes familiar in its fundamentals can still feel unfamiliar in its details. Even our conception of the fundamentals can significantly change over time. Again, I imagine many experienced musicians feel this way.

Through long-term engagement with a pursuit, we develop a rich and personal bond with it. We fill out the dimensions of this bond through the sensations, feelings, and thoughts we experience over time. Each of us undergoes a personal journey with everything we do. It's much harder to feel emotionally rewarded by pursuits we never explore beyond their early stages.

Balancing Novelty and Nuance

This isn't to suggest that the emotional fulfillment gained from long-term pursuits is inherently greater than that which comes from new experiences. They simply scratch different itches; each rewarding in its own way. Ideally, we should aim to experience both. If we want to engage in more long-term pursuits, we need to start choosing activities based on the subtle differences they offer. That selection becomes easier when we train ourselves to appreciate the value of nuance. It's only through extended engagement with a pursuit that we gain the privilege of noticing its finer details.

We may resist pursuing subtly different experiences because of the notion that "life is short" and that we need to "make the most of it". Many people take this to mean trying as many radically different things as possible. This is the wrong way of thinking about it. For me, making the most of life means pursuing whatever best optimizes my satisfaction in the moment. If that means doing something radically different, I'll do that. But if the moment calls for deepening my relationship with something familiar — and experiencing it in a richer, more nuanced, and subtly different way — then that's what I'll pursue instead. Of course, I don't want to miss out on something dramatically distinct, but I also don't want to miss out on rich nuances. I can't have it all, obviously, but I can strike a balance that optimizes my satisfaction in each moment.

It's also worth noting that pursuits we've had a long relationship with can still offer radically different combinations of sensations, emotions, and thoughts — not just subtle ones. While they often seem to provide only subtle variation, the reality is that it's hard to predict. One reason it's hard to anticipate how radically or subtly different our future experiences with a long-term pursuit might be is that our current level of skill limits what we can imagine. For example, someone with a moderate level of skill on an instrument may not yet be able to fully imagine what it feels like to play at a more advanced level. They have to reach that higher level of ability before they can truly grasp the experience it provides.

LIVING MORALLY CAN LEAD TO FULFILLMENT

Whenever we take steps to become someone who is more likely to act consistently with our conscience, we usually find that emotionally rewarding. This includes moments when we:

- Improve our ability to be honest with ourselves when our stated principles don't align with our moral compass.
- Strengthen the impulse to do the right thing. This often requires unlearning egotistic thought patterns that make us more likely to take out our emotional pain on others.
- Increase our willingness to acknowledge that we have the capability, impulse, and desire to act immorally.

All of this can be characterized as a form of us "conquering ourselves". Taking responsibility — whether for our own moral behavior or more generally — is a rewarding goal that is satisfying to strive towards, although difficult at times.

BECOMING OPTIMISTIC

To feel optimistic about life, we need to believe there's a strong likelihood of desirable outcomes in the things we do.

When a person is about to start an endeavor, they think almost only in terms of whether they will get the *final* desired outcome. They often overlook the other valuable outcomes that can arise simply from making the attempt. As mentioned previously, these include us:

- Acquiring new skills or maturing existing ones.

- Having experiences that can be fun, interesting, and engaging.
- Having experiences that pose a different set of challenges to what you're used to.

It's easy to believe that these other desirable outcomes are likely to occur if we move forward with the endeavor. This belief allows us to feel optimistic about those specific outcomes and about the undertaking as a whole. That's how I tend to feel toward everything I attempt, and in turn, it makes me feel quite optimistic about life itself.

When we broaden our optimism to include desirable outcomes in each moment — not just the final result — we can sustain it throughout the experience. We begin to look forward not only to the outcome but also to what unfolds along the way. This creates a steady, stable form of optimism that is both satisfying and motivating. It helps us persevere and remain resilient when challenges arise. By contrast, if our optimism is tied only to the end result, it tends to fluctuate throughout the experience; rising and falling with each obstacle we encounter.

While it's valuable to tie our emotional outlook to the other valuable outcomes that can emerge during an activity, it's also worth strengthening our optimism about reaching the end result we want. My interest in this is in exploring how much of that confidence can be grounded in reason and logic, rather than delusion. While "fake it till you make it" is useful, I don't want it to be my only source of confidence in reaching the outcome I desire.

How optimistic we feel about this final result largely depends on the mental frameworks we've adopted. Two people might do the same endeavor, yet their emotional outlook can differ significantly based on the thought patterns they apply. We'll now examine the patterns that most influence our optimism here.

OPTIMISM BASED ON HOW WE VIEW OUR OWN COMPETENCE

Some people — perhaps without consciously realizing it — base their optimism on the belief that no challenges will arise during the endeavor. But this mindset is flawed, as obstacles often do appear. Telling ourselves they're unlikely is a form of self-deception.

Instead, our confidence should come from believing there's a strong possibility we can overcome those challenges. This is a far more reasonable position; one we can often justify with logic. Whether we hold this belief largely depends on how we perceive our own competence — that is, our skills — to handle these hurdles.

Obviously, it's easier to believe in our competence when it comes to challenges we've been made aware of in advance. When we can see obstacles coming, we're better able to prepare and build the skills needed to overcome them. We might study those challenges before-hand or even do a practice run if possible. Alternatively, we may have already faced similar obstacles in a separate task. And the competence gained from that experience can help us navigate the new one more effectively.

It's harder to believe in our competence when it comes to challenges we haven't yet identified. While we don't have visibility into what these specific obstacles will be, we're aware that they exist and may arise during the task. It's possible we've unwittingly built the necessary skills; perhaps through previous endeavors that, while unrelated, presented similar challenges. However, without clearly identifying these obstacles, it's difficult to confidently say we're prepared for them, whether intentionally or unwittingly.

Belief in Our Ability to Improvise

That being said, even without having prepared for a specific obstacle, we may still overcome it. In such cases, we rely on our ability to improvise — that is, to quickly identify the nature of a problem and solve it without prior planning. This is a skill of spontaneous problem-solving and navigating issues intuitively. So even if we're not competent through preparation, we may still be competent through our improvisational ability.

I think many of us lack confidence in our ability to improvise. This often stems from early conditioning that taught us to rely almost entirely on preparation to solve problems. Much of this conditioning took place in school, where most exams focused on testing our ability to memorize and recall information. In that environment, success was based more on preparation than on our capacity to adapt or think on our feet.

Due to this repeated conditioning over more than a decade, I believe many of us became *comfortable* only with solving problems we had been specifically prepared for. We tend to think that, in order to solve a problem, we must first be shown how to do it. As a result, we've grown uncomfortable with situations that require improvisation. This is why, when faced with an unexpected problem, we often assume we can't overcome it.

To be clear, I'm not suggesting that the current education system lacks value or that people shouldn't go to school. I bring this up because I think it's helpful to understand why we may lack confidence in our ability to improvise. Whether as children or adults, we should work to build trust in our capacity to solve problems on the spot, rather than relying solely on planning. By developing this confidence, we strengthen our belief that we can handle unanticipated challenges that arise during an endeavor. In doing so, we cultivate greater optimism about reaching the desired end result.

We Often Underestimate Our Improvisational Ability

I think we're generally quite decent at improvising through the problems we face. After all, we regularly deal with situations we didn't prepare for or anticipate. In these moments, we have no choice but to think on our feet in order to solve the issue. In reality, we've been training this skillset continuously. We just haven't framed it as "improvisation".

In my view, while we may lack confidence in our ability to spontaneously problem-solve, we don't necessarily lack the competence. Of course, this skill can always be improved, and some people are better at specific types of improvisation than others — but overall, I think most of us are generally decent. By recognizing that we're developing this ability all the time, we can begin to build greater confidence in it.

The value of having confidence in this ability cannot be overstated. I believe many of us already have enough of this skill to handle most of the difficult, unanticipated challenges we face. But when we lack confidence in that ability, we're more likely to panic or freeze, making it harder to overcome the obstacle.

By contrast, someone with the same level of improvisational ability but greater self-confidence tends to be much more solution-oriented when faced with unexpected challenges. They're more likely to overcome the obstacle simply because they trust themselves to handle it. I don't believe the people we see as highly successful in reaching their desired outcomes necessarily have superior improvisational skills. At least, not by a wide margin anyway. What sets them apart is their confidence in that ability. When an unanticipated challenge arises, they don't panic and freeze; they have confidence in themselves and try to tackle it head-on.

Becoming More Open to Attempting Things Without Much Information

When we're conditioned to rely solely on preparation to solve problems, we may become less willing to attempt things where we lack prior information. Faced with a task we understand little about, we might assume there are too many unidentified challenges we can't adequately prepare for. In some situations, this caution might be responsible. But in many cases, I think we should still give such endeavors a go, even if we have only limited information about what obstacles may arise.

This is for a couple of key reasons.

First, most of us possess sufficient improvisational ability to overcome many of the challenges that do come up. We would succeed at getting past these obstacles more often than we might expect. We're a lot more ready than we think, even without planning.

Second, even if we don't overcome the challenges or attain the desired result, the attempt itself can still lead to valuable outcomes. As mentioned, this includes experiences that are interesting, fun, and engaging. Some of these we can anticipate and others we can't. We shouldn't miss out on these.

What helps us become more comfortable attempting endeavors with limited information is, of course, developing our general improvisational ability and building confidence in it. A key way to strengthen this skill is by training our mind to first identify the basic principles underlying any given task. These principles offer guidance on what we're fundamentally aiming for in the activity and typically apply across most — if not all — of its moments. When an unanticipated challenge arises, keeping such guidance in mind makes it easier to figure out a solution.

OPTIMISM BASED ON HOW WE VIEW OUR OWN LUCK

In any activity, getting to the desired outcome always involves some combination of our own competence and luck. No matter how skilled we are, there will always be factors outside our control that can prevent us from reaching the final result.

When we are "lucky" during an undertaking, such factors happen to arrange themselves in a way that helps us. Or at least does not obstruct our progress. When we are "not lucky", such factors align in ways that do not help and may even hinder us from attaining the result we desire. Regardless of how competent we are, we still rely on luck to get us the rest of the way.

Although every endeavor requires some combination of competence and luck to attain the desired result, the *degree of each can vary*. For tasks that demand high competence, we need to believe we possess that competence in order to feel confident about our chances. Similarly, when success depends heavily on luck, we must believe we're fortunate enough to expect a favorable outcome. While we can more logically justify a belief in our own competence, it's much harder to do so with respect to how lucky we are. In my view, claiming to be "lucky" quickly ventures into superstition. Belief in our own luck isn't grounded in anything logical.

The Extent to Which We Can Logically Justify Our Luck

So, is there a way to logically increase our optimism about attaining a desired result when it depends heavily on luck? I would say yes, but it only takes us so far. There are two things we can do.

The first is to develop our competence in the area as much as possible. Whether by preparing more thoroughly or honing improvisational skills suited to the task. Doing so increases our chances of reaching the desired outcome. That said, there is a limit to how much we can use our own competence to increase our luck.

The second is not to believe that we are always lucky, but to believe in the *possibility that we are in this instance*. This means holding the view that, in this attempt, it's possible the factors align in our favor, allowing us to reach the desired outcome. Even if the odds are statistically low, they may happen to favor us this time. In my view, this belief, while only different in a subtle way, is easier to justify logically.

OPTIMISM THROUGH CHALLENGING OUR EGO

Our ego can make us worry about looking foolish for being optimistic. When this concern is present, it becomes harder to believe we have a strong chance of reaching our desired outcome. In this way, our optimism can be inhibited by the ego.

Our ego can have this inhibiting effect even when we have a strong logical basis for believing we're competent enough to overcome the obstacles ahead. Ideally, our assessment of how likely we are to reach the desired outcome should be grounded in our view of our own competence, since that framework is rooted in logic. In contrast, when the ego interferes, it undermines this assessment not through reason, but through paranoia and fear. The more we let our ego weigh in on our assessment of the chances, the more we allow that assessment to be driven by paranoia rather than logic.

Many people who don't consider themselves optimistic about attaining desired outcomes see their stance as well-reasoned. They think they have a very logical basis for not being optimistic. Maybe there are instances when they do, but I suspect that, in many cases, their outlook is heavily influenced by their ego's fear of looking foolish.

We should take steps to remove the ego's influence from our assessment of how likely we are to reach a desired outcome. Without that interference, we're more likely to base our evaluation on our actual competence, making it easier to feel genuinely optimistic. That said, there may still be situations where, even with the ego set aside, we assess the likelihood of success as low based on an honest evaluation of our abilities. In those cases, at least our lack of optimism is grounded in logic, not egotistic fear.

How to Remove the Ego's Influence on Our Optimism

We remove this influence by getting the ego to stop worrying about looking foolish for being optimistic about attaining the final desired outcome. But how do we actually do that?

Once again, we have to convince the ego that this way of thinking belongs to the *greater fool*. It's a mindset that can cause us to miss out on final desired outcomes we were actually capable of reaching. Since our ego did not want us to be optimistic, it stopped us from recognizing the competence we actually had. As a result, we might not even attempt the task. Or if we do, we give up as soon as we encounter a challenge.

Because of the ego's concern with appearing foolish to others, we miss out on achieving the final desired outcomes of many potential endeavors. This is exactly what the greater fool misses out on. And for all the things we chose not to try, we also forgo the other valuable outcomes we could have experienced in the attempt. As mentioned, this includes moments that might have been fun, interesting, and engaging.

When our ego becomes overly concerned with appearing foolish for being optimistic about reaching the final desired outcome, it can lead to what I call "default pessimism". In this state, our baseline assumption — for most things we do, or perhaps everything — is that we're unlikely to succeed. We don't even take the time to logically assess whether we're actually competent. This default pessimism reflects the mindset of the greater fool, as it can cause us to miss out on so many opportunities across all areas of life.

Once we've dismantled the ego's worry, we should no longer feel foolish for being optimistic about reaching the desired end result. And without the ego, we also shouldn't feel foolish even if we were optimistic and still didn't attain the final outcome we wanted. After all, when we believe we have a strong likelihood of getting this end result, we are still allowing for the possibility that we won't. So, not reaching the outcome remains within the range of possibilities we expected.

Even if I did still feel silly for being optimistic and not getting the result, I'd rather be that kind of fool than the far greater one. This is the one so afraid of appearing silly for being optimistic that they miss out on all the satisfying experiences they could have had in the attempt. Some people think it's foolish to try. I think it's foolish not to.

THE TWO TYPES OF OPTIMISM WE CAN FEEL

These are the feelings of "calm optimism" and "excited optimism". With the calm version, we're still enthusiastic, but not in a way that's bursting or overflowing like the excited kind. While the excited version feels like out-of-control enthusiasm, the calm one feels very nice and even-keeled. It's still very satisfying and very enjoyable.

For me, I generally experience calm optimism with respect to my undertakings. I feel this way even if I strongly believe in the likelihood of getting the final desired outcome. I do experience the excited version a fair bit, but I do not regard it as something I need to be having all the time. It's a nice-to-have as opposed to being essential.

FEELING PESSIMISTIC SHOULDN'T ALWAYS MEAN WE'RE SUFFERING

When we don't believe there's a strong chance of getting the final desired outcome, we tend to feel pessimistic about it. This feeling is not intrinsically one of suffering. It can be "emotionally neutral" — neither satisfying nor dissatisfying. At times, it can even be satisfying to the part of us that enjoys a challenge, like playing a game where the odds are stacked against us.

Many of us mistake the feeling of pessimism for emotional suffering. This confusion often arises because we apply mental frameworks that cause us to suffer emotionally when we don't get the desired end result. For example:

- Our ego being attached to the power to get the final result. What we mistake for the feeling of pessimism is the ego-created powerlessness, helplessness, and anger.
- Our belief that it is impossible to be happy unless we get this end outcome. What we call the feeling of pessimism is actually the despair caused to us by this conditional belief about happiness.

Two people can both feel pessimistic about their low chances of getting the final desired outcome, but only the one who applies those mental frameworks will emotionally suffer. Feeling pessimistic doesn't have to snowball into suffering.

There are other things we should prevent our pessimistic beliefs from snowballing into. We should not let such pessimism demotivate us to the point where we don't even make an attempt. Again, even if we don't reach the final desired outcome, we can still have fun, interesting, and engaging experiences throughout the endeavor. We might try something despite feeling pessimistic, but that pessimism can hold us back from fully engaging or reduce the effort we put in. We should work to prevent this as well.

BECOMING OPTIMISTIC ABOUT THE REALIZATION OF OUR IDEALS

Some people think it is foolish to have ideals. They believe that striving for them can only lead to despair, since reality will never fully measure up. They equate this pursuit with suffering. However, contrary to popular belief, we don't feel despair simply because we haven't attained what we envision. No — it arises because we have adopted a happiness conditional statement that stipulates we cannot be happy if this ideal is unmet.

Recognizing that the despair comes from this conditional belief allows us to discard it. Going forward, we can acknowledge where reality falls short of our vision without experiencing this distress. Even if the universe is somehow structured against the full realization of what we value, we can still find a way to be happy. To be clear, it's not that I've let go of these aspirations or no longer care about them. I do — and I still want to see them realized — but I will not despair when they are not.

Simply having ideals and *living in the spirit of them* can be satisfying. It is this enjoyable feeling that can motivate us to bring beneficial transformations to reality. Even if we don't fully realize the vision, there is something satisfying in bringing reality that much closer to it. Even if it involves a lot of discomfiture and effort, I still want to do it. I'm curious how close I can get.

How Can We Become More Optimistic About Our Ideals Being Realized?

It's difficult to believe there's a strong likelihood of *fully* attaining what we envision. I don't think we can really change what we honestly believe on that point. We can, however, believe there is a strong chance of realizing our ideals in ways we find enjoyable on some level — even if only partially attained. In that sense, I am optimistic about the pursuit.

There are two core ideals that I believe are worthwhile for everyone to pursue.

One is being able to more easily enter the mental state that is optimal for engaging with each moment of reality. As in, the playful mind. In this state, we're better able to draw happiness and contentment from each point in time.

The other ideal is making the world a better place. To me, that means increasing overall satisfaction and reducing suffering, whether physical or emotional. Even if we improve someone's experience by just a little, we've still made a real, material difference. Even if it's only for one person, in one moment. And even if that person is you. I think the vast majority of us contribute in this way every day.

9

THE COMPULSION
TO CONTINUE LIVING

I call it a "compulsion" to keep living because we continue existing even when part of us wants to stop. This compulsion can be overridden if the desire to not live becomes strong enough, but usually, it keeps us alive despite those feelings. Simply wanting to stop living is generally not enough to end our existence. Something compels us to carry on.

THE TWO COMPULSIONS TO CONTINUE

In my view, we have two forces that compel us to keep living.

First, there is a *biological* compulsion to survive that exists independently of any reasons we might have for living. No matter what reasons we articulate to ourselves about why we should go on, there is always an underlying biological drive pushing us to continue. This compulsion was especially evident when we were children; back then, it kept us going even before we had fully formed reasons to live. This strong biological drive persists into adulthood.

Secondly, when we develop reasons to live, this creates a *mental* compulsion to continue living. At its core, the fundamental reason is simply, "I want to live because I want to live". This basic reason doesn't really disappear, so there is always a mental drive to keep going. Beyond this core reason, we often find additional reasons to exist, usually related to pursuing fulfilling and satisfying experiences. Each additional reason can *strengthen* this mental compulsion.

In contrast to our biological and mental compulsions to stay alive, we can also develop a mental force pushing us to stop living. This force often emerges during intense emotional suffering or when our capacity for satisfaction is deeply blocked. More specifically, it arises from mental frameworks we've adopted that cause pain and hinder our enjoyment. This inner pressure fuels the desire to die. By unlearning these harmful frameworks, we weaken that force and with it, the desire to stop living.

Clarifying the Desire to Die

There are key aspects of this desire worth understanding so we can better respond to it. These are based on my own experiences with suicidal ideation, which I appreciate may not reflect everyone else's.

First, wanting to die is not necessarily the same as wanting to kill ourselves. We may wish to die, but that doesn't always mean we want to take active steps to make it happen. For example, we might hope a bus would hit us, but we won't necessarily step in front of one. The wish to die develops into an urge to end our own life when the thought patterns we've adopted cause *even more* intense emotional pain. This heightened suffering creates such a strong mental force to stop living that the impulse to take action arises. By clearing away these harmful frameworks, we not only free ourselves from the pain but also lessen the urge to end our lives.

Second, any urge to die or end our lives represents only *a part of us.* This part *coexists simultaneously* alongside other, more fundamental parts that still want to live. When we experience the wish to die or harm ourselves, we often mistakenly believe it means no aspect of us wants to keep going. That isn't true. Both opposing urges can be present at the same time. While we may want to end our lives because of the suffering we feel, we can still hold reasons to keep living. As mentioned earlier, these reasons often involve the desire to explore fulfilling experiences. The core reason — "I want to live because I want to live" — should persist despite the pain. When coming across the desire to die, we should avoid panicking and assuming that we have no desire to live.

We also should not panic or assume that having the urge to end our lives means we will act on it. The mental force pushing us to stop living coexists with our biological and mental compulsions to keep going. As long as these compulsions remain stronger than the urge to die, we won't take steps to harm ourselves. When the urge to die becomes stronger, however, we may act on it. To keep our biological and mental drives stronger, we need to dismantle the mental frameworks that block our contentment and cause us pain.

When Suicidal Ideation Is Present but Not Overwhelming

After unlearning the painful frameworks, we might still notice a part of us that wants to die or harm ourselves. Even if we're not feeling intense emotional distress, these urges can linger somewhat. Depending on the situation, if the desire to end our lives appears only occasionally and isn't very strong, I wouldn't be too concerned about it.

I believe it's difficult to completely eliminate these parts of ourselves once they've formed. For me, such thoughts still surface occasionally, even when I'm not actively suffering. To be clear, I'm not discouraging anyone from seeking professional help if needed. I'm simply suggesting that we avoid panicking or overreacting when we notice occasional suicidal thoughts, as long as they're not driven by intense emotional pain.

One thing we should avoid is adopting any happiness conditional statements that make us think it's impossible to be happy because of suicidal tendencies. This belief can create unnecessary despair that may actually strengthen what would otherwise be low-level suicidal thoughts. When we notice urges to die or end our lives, we should remind ourselves that happiness is still possible. Not only in the future but also in the present. Just because one part of us struggles with suicidal thoughts doesn't mean the rest of us can't experience happiness. These experiences aren't mutually exclusive; they can coexist.

MENTAL FRAMEWORKS THAT STRONGLY DRIVE SUICIDAL IDEATION

While any mental framework that causes pain can contribute to suicidal ideation, some cause especially intense suffering and therefore have the greatest influence on suicidal thoughts. There are two in particular that we should have a keen interest in dismantling.

The Ego's Attachment to Control

This first type we've already discussed at considerable length. The ego's attachment to forms of control can cause intense emotional pain. Our ego can care so deeply about these things that it may drive us to consider ending our lives over not having them. I attribute most of my past suicidal tendencies to a mismanaged ego. We can help our ego detach from these forms of control by asking whether they're honestly worth killing ourselves over.

From my experience with suicidal thoughts, I've found that the cause is not only emotional suffering but also the belief that I'm powerless over that pain. This belief amplifies my ego's feelings of helplessness. When I recognized that my suffering came entirely from mental frameworks I had adopted, I realized I was both the cause and the one in control. I am responsible for my own suicidal tendencies. I just need to understand how to dismantle these thought patterns to ease the emotional distress. This realization helped address my ego's concerns about lacking control and, as a result, reduced my feelings of helplessness.

A Nihilistic Outlook

There are many versions of nihilism, but it generally comes down to the belief that "nothing matters". We've already covered a few of its central arguments in Chapters 1 and 7, though I avoided using the term "nihilism" back then since it can be a big topic and wasn't the main focus. This perspective is important to challenge because it can be particularly corrosive to the desire to do anything, including the desire to live.

My main counter to nihilism is that every moment matters because each one impacts our satisfaction. Therefore, everything we do in these moments matters as well. I will now recap the other arguments put forward by nihilism, along with their counterpoints:

- Nothing matters to the universe: we cannot demonstrate what does or does not matter to it. Even if we could, we should remain indifferent to what the universe thinks.
- Nothing matters because we will eventually die and won't be remembered: avoiding death or seeking to be remembered aren't the only reasons to act. I act because I'm caught in the present moment and trying to enjoy it.
- There is no meaning, purpose, or point of life: there is actually an abundance of meaning, purpose and points in every moment of our lives.

As an additional counterpoint, I'd ask nihilists to honestly consider how they would react if punched in the face without provocation. Or if someone stole something from them. Most would likely feel anger. Why react this way if they genuinely believed that nothing mattered? They get angry because that punch or that theft affects their satisfaction and causes suffering — things they care about.

Given all this, I find it logically impossible to be nihilistic, though that wasn't always the case. For many years, I had a very nihilistic outlook.

Some nihilists adopt the view that because nothing matters, it grants them the freedom to do anything. I have a few challenges to this. While that view may seem to grant freedom, it will also kill their motivation to do any of it. After all, why would you bother doing anything when you think it doesn't matter? In addition, I don't see this perspective as ultimately offering more freedom than the view that every moment matters.

Even if we no longer believe in nihilism, we might still feel that way. These feelings can remain unpleasant, sometimes leading to despair. They are largely influenced by how we think about ourselves experiencing "nothingness". We will explore how to address these thoughts in the next section.

LOGICALLY, IS IT POSSIBLE FOR US TO EXPERIENCE "NOTHINGNESS" IN LIFE?

I would assert that it is *not* logically possible for us to experience "nothingness" while we are alive. Therefore, any despair related to this is entirely unnecessary.

It all comes down to how we define "nothing". For me, nothing means the complete absence of something. With this in mind, it's impossible for us to experience nothing, since *experience itself is fundamentally a form of something*. This experience can always be described more specifically in terms of our sensations, emotions, and thoughts. That we can describe the attributes of every experience suggests that, at its essence, experience is a form of something. It is never a form of nothing.

It's also easy to see *each moment* as a form of something. As mentioned earlier, each moment consists of the sensorial, emotional, and conceptual experiences we observe at that point in time. Since every instant is made up entirely of experience, it is always composed of "something". The specifics of that "something" may change from one moment to the next, and we may not fully grasp its nature each time — but that "something" is always present. We never experience "nothingness" in any moment, as it is logically impossible. Not even to the slightest degree. "Nothingness" simply doesn't fit within our model of reality.

The experiences we often label as "nothing" have actually been forms of something all along. We will now explore common experiences that are frequently mischaracterized as "nothing" and identify the attributes that reveal them as forms of something. What we'll find is that these experiences become less emotionally unpleasant when we view them as "something" rather than "nothing". This shift in framing significantly changes how we feel about them. Some are only unpleasant because we mistakenly see them as "nothing".

Empty Space

To observe an empty space — like an empty box or an empty room — we have to *see* it. This empty space is a form of something as we experience it visually.

Darkness

Darkness is also a form of something by virtue of us being able to experience it visually.

A Feeling of Being Unfulfilled

As a reminder, the feeling of being unfulfilled arises when we expect more or longer-lasting fulfillment than we actually receive. When we let go of that expectation, the distress disappears.

Sometimes, when feeling unfulfilled, we describe ourselves as "feeling nothing". To me, this is illogical. Feeling nothing would mean the complete absence of all emotion. Yet being unfulfilled is a feeling itself. While we may be missing the emotion of fulfillment, we're not empty of feeling entirely. We are clearly still experiencing something.

A Feeling That Doesn't Fit Into Common Emotional Categories

Sometimes we experience feelings that don't seem to fit into common emotional categories like love, hate, happiness, or sadness. These unclassified feelings can be subtle, mixed, and more neutral compared to the broader emotions.

We might assume that the only emotions that exist are these broader categories. Because of this assumption, we may mistakenly label subtle, mixed, and neutral feelings as "feelings of nothingness". But this is illogical. Again, it's not an absence of all feeling. We are obviously experiencing *something*. It just doesn't fit into any of the broader categories we typically recognize.

How should we describe these feelings if they don't fit into broader categories and it's illogical to call them "feelings of nothingness"? Usually, it's quite difficult to find precise words for subtle emotions. Often, the best we can do is use terms that describe them to *some degree*. For me, words like "subtle", "muddled", and "middle-of-the-road" work well. Even saying they "don't fit into the broader categories of emotion" is a more accurate description than calling them "nothing".

Describing any feeling as a "feeling of nothingness" can lead us to react to it with fear. This framing can turn a subtle emotion that wasn't especially uncomfortable or unpleasant into a source of suffering. Over time, we may become so used to fearing this subtle feeling that we start to believe it is inherently painful, even while paradoxically calling it a "feeling of nothingness". When we remove this "nothing" framing, the fear fades. We then discover that this emotion is not inherently a source of distress or dissatisfaction.

We may also react to this subtle emotion with fear because we don't understand what it is or why we're feeling it. This fear, born from our lack of comprehension, can turn the underlying emotion into suffering. But this response is entirely unnecessary. We only fear what we don't understand because we've been conditioned to do so. Instead, we can train ourselves to respond calmly when encountering something unfamiliar. Not everything unfamiliar needs to be treated as a threat.

When we fear any feeling — whether subtle or intense — we instinctively resist it, wanting it to go away. Ironically, this very fear and resistance cause it to linger. By fearing it, we give it the attention that keeps it alive. By resisting it, we block its passage on the way out. Instead of fearing or resisting these feelings, we should learn to respect them and get out of its way. When we do, they often pass on their own or quietly fade into the background.

Activities Which We Frame as Forms of "Doing Nothing"

Framing any activity as a form of "doing nothing" is completely illogical. If we are doing any kind of action, it is clearly a form of something. Even sitting and relaxing are still forms of doing something.

Is there ever a moment while we're alive when we aren't doing any activity, and thus doing nothing? No — because at any given time, we are always at least doing the following:

- We undergo biological and chemical processes that keep us alive, such as electrical signals passing through the brain and nervous system and the heart pumping blood throughout the body.
- We are sensorially, emotionally, and conceptually experiencing something.
- We are optimizing our satisfaction.

Since we are always doing these activities, we are always doing something and never nothing. Even when we are just *being*.

When We Frame the Self as a Form of "Nothing"

When we frame the self as "nothing", what we really mean is that we don't believe the self exists. To me, this is illogical because the self is clearly an experience and therefore a form of something. We can describe this "something" in detail by looking at the combination of sensations, emotions, and thoughts that make up the self at any given moment. If the self did not exist and were genuinely "nothing", we wouldn't be able to describe its attributes in this way.

What leads us to frame the self as "nothing" in the first place? Why do we think it doesn't exist? Many of us arrive at this conclusion when we struggle to find a *baseline* definition of the self that is logically consistent with our observed experiences. While we can identify specific traits — like the food and music we enjoy — it often feels like a random collection of qualities rather than a cohesive description of what the self fundamentally is.

The difficulty in finding this baseline definition can lead us to assume that the self simply does not exist. My views on this basic conceptualization are detailed in Chapter 5. Once we grasp that, we can deepen our understanding of the self by exploring the specific sensations, emotions, and thoughts we experience.

We might also question the existence of the self when we can't identify a fundamental narrative or roles that make sense based on our experiences. In my view, we're all part of the "saga of optimizing satisfaction through self-actualization", as discussed in Chapter 7. Within this narrative, we play the core role of the experiencer, who combines the qualities of the scientist, the warrior, and the craftsman to optimize well-being. While we may take on other roles or explore different combinations, we never cease to be the experiencer.

The final reason we might doubt the existence of the self is that we seek a definition we can prove to be true. With this mindset, we only accept the self's existence if we find a definition that can be proven with 100% certainty. The problem is that we can never prove anything conclusively, since unobserved factors might always contradict our beliefs. As a result, we may encounter a definition of the self that we honestly believe is logically consistent with our experiences so far, but because we cannot prove it definitively, we reject it. When we let go of the need for absolute proof, we can more readily accept a definition of the self that we honestly believe aligns logically with our experience.

It's possible that we frame other foundational building blocks of reality as "nothing" for similar reasons — such as life, morality, and the fundamental narrative. We struggle to find baseline definitions for these, or we only accept ones we can prove with 100% certainty. When so many core foundations of our reality are labeled as "nothing", it greatly intensifies our feelings of nothingness. But when we recognize that they are all forms of something, that feeling begins to dissipate, and we feel much more grounded and oriented.

Death

All the examples we've discussed above are experiences we have *while alive*. Each is a form of something, making it illogical to describe them as "nothing". But what about when we are dead? Can death be framed as "experiencing nothing" then?

To answer this question, we need a clearer grasp of what physically happens in the brain during the transition from life to death. In each moment we are alive, we have electrical signals being generated inside there. It is because these electrical signals are being generated that we are *experiencing* at that point in time. The last electrical signal we ever produce in the brain contains the last combination of sensations, emotions, and thoughts we ever experience. This is our last moment alive.

Beyond that final moment, no electrical signals are produced in the brain. At this point, we no longer have the *ability to experience* because we no longer exist. Some people interpret this to mean that, when we are dead, we are simply looking at literal darkness. But this is impossible, since we no longer have functioning eyes or electrical signals in our brains. The best way to think about what it's like to be dead is to consider what it was like before we were born. During that time, we didn't exist and therefore could not experience anything. It wasn't as if we were perceiving darkness the whole time. We just simply *weren't*. Death, I suspect, would be the same thing. We just won't be.

Death is not an experience. Life is an experience. And the last moment we experience is of us being alive. After that final moment, we are dead and we stop experiencing. We can, of course, experience the *process of dying* leading up to our last moment alive, but we never experience death itself. This makes me much less afraid of it, as I see little point in fearing something I will never experience. We're not even going to be aware that we're dead. The notion of death is still somewhat scary to me on some level given how unfathomable it is, but I am much calmer about it. It allows me to spend more time enjoying life instead of worrying about death and what it might be like. I can focus more on being the experiencer.

It is also worth noting that our *experience* of our fundamental narrative does not end in death. It ends in life, with the last moment in that narrative still being a living one. From our perspective, the story begins with life and ends with life. Only the people around us who are alive after we are gone will view our story as ending in death.

Challenging the Assumption That "Nothingness" Is the Default State

We've often been taught to think that nothingness is the default state of existence, and that "something" is the exception. This notion is implicit in the classic question: *why is there something instead of nothing?*

That question assumes there must be a reason for something to exist, but no reason is required for nothing to exist. We find it difficult to accept that the universe simply *is*, yet we don't struggle in the same way to accept that if there were nothing, no explanation would be needed.

But why do we assume that nothingness is the default? If we look at the universe around us, there's far more evidence suggesting that *something is the inherent state*. Simply by virtue of all this something existing, while nothing does not.

10

TRAITS THAT ARE VITAL TO SATISFYING RELATIONSHIPS

Why understand this? There are two reasons.

Firstly, a key part of optimizing our satisfaction is having relationships that are fulfilling, whether they be romantic, familial, or friendly. The more we learn how to improve the quality of these relationships, the greater our overall satisfaction.

Secondly, as previously discussed, it is a foundational building block in our model of reality. Without sufficiently grasping this, we find it hard to engage with what's right in front of us.

Satisfaction is best cultivated in a relationship when the parties involved possess the following traits:

- They recognize the fundamental qualities they share with each other.
- They adhere to the golden rule of treating others as they would like to be treated.
- They focus not only on improving the relationship with each other but also their relationships with themselves.

The more we develop these traits in our relationships, the more satisfying those relationships become. However, obstacles often arise that make strengthening these traits challenging. In this chapter, we'll explore these attributes in greater detail and discuss how to overcome the barriers that stand in our way.

EACH PERSON RECOGNIZES THE FUNDAMENTAL QUALITIES THEY SHARE WITH EACH OTHER

Recognizing fundamental similarities with another person fosters a satisfying sense of closeness and oneness. The more similarities we identify, the stronger the emotional connection grows.

For me, the most fundamental of these similarities emerge when we articulate the "baseline definition of the self". This baseline self includes the attributes we share with every other human being. This makes these traits universal and not limited to a subset of humanity. As discussed in Chapter 5, the baseline self comprises the following attributes:

- *The self is an experience.* We all fundamentally experience reality in the same way — that is, through sensations, emotions, and thoughts.
- The self fundamentally wants to optimize our well-being. Each of us seeks sensorial and emotional gratification while avoiding sensorial and emotional pain. We are all fundamentally driven by the same core desire.
- The self can be articulated in terms of the "present self", "past self", and "future self". Each of us experiences different versions of the self over time, with every version utterly unique in its sensations, emotions, and thoughts. In each moment, we all experience reality through the present self.

When we understand the baseline self we all share, we become more comfortable embracing the differences between us. No matter how much we may differ on the surface, something fundamental will always connect us — in who we are and how we experience reality.

These distinctions between people exist not in the fundamentals, but in the *details*. For example, while we all sense, feel, and think, the specific sensations, feelings, and thoughts we have at any moment can differ. Additionally, although we all want to optimize our well-being, the specific types of emotional enjoyment we seek can vary.

As we examine these details, it becomes easier to appreciate how genuinely unique each person is. While the combination of sensations, feelings, and thoughts someone else experiences may resemble our own in some ways, it is never exactly the same.

Seeing these similarities helps us understand the other person in a fundamental way. As we learn the specific details of who they are, what they want, and what they experience, we grasp them in a more detailed way. Comprehending what another person senses, feels, and thinks can be deeply satisfying.

Can We Prove Our Understanding of Another Person with 100% Certainty?

No — just as we can't prove anything we understand is 100% true, we can't prove our view of another person is either. This includes both the baseline self we see as shared by all humans and the unique details we learn about each individual. All we can do is form a conception of the other person that we honestly believe is logically consistent with what we've observed so far.

The difficulty of proving our conception becomes clearer when we realize that each individual directly experiences only their own sensations, feelings, and thoughts. This is an inner world inaccessible to others. We can only *infer* another person's inner experience based on their words and actions.

When forming our view of another person, we rely largely on our understanding of ourselves. We tend to *assume* that what we gather about ourselves is likely similar for other people, simply because they are also human beings. In other words, we use our own sensations, feelings, and thoughts to define the baseline self because that's all we have direct access to. Since we cannot directly observe anyone else's inner experience, different people can have varying baseline definitions of the self. Moreover, when our conception of ourselves changes, it can alter our baseline definition of the self and, in turn, our conception of others. In this way, we use ourselves as an "identity template" to understand other people.

We do not assume the other person is exactly the same as us. Instead, we tend to recognize fundamental similarities while allowing for differences in the details. These similarities and differences become apparent through observing what they say and do. We attribute these similarities and differences to the biological and environmental factors that have shaped both them and us.

We can still feel closeness and oneness with someone even if we don't believe we comprehend them completely or with certainty. We just have to honestly think we grasp them *well enough.*

What Leads Someone to Misrepresent Themselves to Others

Our understanding of who another person is — including what they sense, feel, and think — depends largely on what they tell us. A person can only communicate what they are aware of themselves and cannot speak to aspects beyond their awareness. In such cases, we can encourage them to be more introspective. The more they understand themselves, the more they can share. At the very least, helping them articulate their sensations, feelings, and thoughts better can benefit both the relationship and their own self-awareness.

Sometimes the issue isn't a lack of self-awareness. It could be that the person is intentionally presenting a version of themselves they don't honestly believe in. They are deliberately misrepresenting who they are.

One of the main reasons someone does this is due to self-esteem issues. It's not necessarily driven by malice. They may have been conditioned from a young age to believe they are fundamentally worthless and to link their personal value to how impressed others are with them. More details on how this conditioning occurs can be found in Chapter 2. As a result, this person says whatever they think will impress others, even if it misrepresents what they genuinely believe about themselves.

Thinking someone is impressed *shields* their conscious mind from feeling worthless, but this feeling isn't eliminated. It's merely suppressed in the subconscious. To keep these emotions from surfacing, the person must continuously reinforce this belief in their mind. It would take less effort for them to let go of the idea that they are fundamentally worthless.

If we're in a relationship with someone who holds this belief, we can help them discard this self-perception. The details on how to do this were discussed in Chapter 2. Once they've let go of this belief, they should more easily discover their innate self-value that was always there but hard to "hear". By finding this, they will no longer tie their personal worth to whether others are impressed and, as a result, should stop misrepresenting themselves due to self-esteem issues.

It's possible that a person deceives their conscious mind into believing they have desirable qualities they don't sincerely believe they possess. Their subconscious is aware of how they honestly see themselves, but they lack the mental fortitude to face this consciously. When they lie to others about themselves, it's primarily because they are lying to themselves first. We should encourage them to build the mental strength needed to confront and accept their honest beliefs about who they are.

The Way That Dishonesty Undermines Shared Moments

When either person in a relationship misrepresents themselves, it deprives both of an enjoyable experience I call the "honest moment". This moment occurs when both parties *genuinely intend* to share how they honestly see themselves. Neither should try to present something that differs from their innermost perception. In these honest moments, there's a satisfying sense of progress as we develop a deeper mutual understanding that is more likely to align with reality. While we can't prove these conceptions of each other are true, the likelihood improves when both strive for sincere self-representation.

When one person mischaracterizes themselves, there's a high chance the other will sense it. They pick up on logical inconsistencies in what's being said and may notice a lack of sincerity through tone, body language, facial expressions, and other subtle cues. Often, this awareness starts subconsciously. We can't immediately pinpoint what feels off. Over time, these feelings become clearer as the inconsistencies and insincerity become more apparent and easier to articulate. Even before we become fully aware at a conscious level, our brain signals that something isn't right. This disrupts the experience of an honest moment, leaving us without the satisfying sense of progress. Deep down, we don't believe we're forming an accurate view of the other person and recognize that no insight can be gained here.

Just to be clear: a genuine intention to accurately represent ourselves does not require revealing everything about ourselves. To have an honest moment, one simply needs to share what is *material* to the conversation at hand. There is no need to disclose what is not. If we detect that the other person holds a mistaken view of us, we should generally correct them to preserve the honesty of the interaction. Whether the correction casts us in a favorable or unfavorable light should largely be irrelevant.

Of course, there may be things about ourselves that we want to keep private, even if they are relevant to the conversation but not strongly relevant to the other person's interests. Everyone has aspects they prefer to keep private. In such cases, we should generally decline to answer by saying something like "that's something I want to keep private", rather than lie outright.

EACH PERSON TREATS OTHERS AS THEY WOULD LIKE TO BE TREATED

As discussed in Chapter 6, "treating others as they would like to be treated" is a general principle embedded in nearly everyone's conscience. This is also referred to as the "golden rule".

According to this principle, an action is considered wrong if we wouldn't want it done to us. When both parties act according to this principle, the relationship becomes more satisfying in three key ways.

First, both parties are less likely to do anything the other would consider wrong.

Second, being in a relationship with someone who consistently follows this principle makes it much easier to like and respect them. We feel this way towards them because it takes self-honesty and effort to recognize and manage impulses to violate this principle. Similarly, when we do the same, the other person will also like and respect us.

Third, when we're in relationships with people who also treat others as they would like to be treated, we can help each other better adhere to this principle. We can encourage greater self-honesty in recognizing when an action conflicts with the principle and support each other in managing our impulses. Through these interactions, we help one another become more like the people we ultimately want to be. Being in such a relationship can be very fulfilling and enjoyable.

Why a Person Does Not Treat Others as They Would Like to Be Treated

I believe the vast majority of people share the golden rule. Yet many still act inconsistently with it, doing things to others they wouldn't want done to themselves. This includes actions that are obviously wrong, such as lying, stealing, and violence. There are three reasons for this. Some have already been discussed in Chapter 6 and are being recapped here.

Firstly, they lack the mental fortitude to honestly accept that they have the capability, impulse, and desire to do the wrong thing. When they feel this impulse, they deceive themselves by convincing themselves they have a "justification" that cancels out the wrongness. These justifications are usually self-deceptions, since if someone else did the same action to them with the same excuse, they would consider it immoral.

Secondly, they are not effective at managing their impulses. They don't take steps to weaken the urge to do the wrong thing or challenge the belief that doing so will lead to happiness. They don't dismantle mental frameworks that cause emotional suffering, which they might then take out on others. They don't manage their ego, nor do they actively strengthen the impulse to do the right thing. They don't recognize how acting consistently with their conscience ultimately helps them like, respect, and find peace with themselves.

Thirdly, they may recognize the golden rule as an important general principle, but *not as their main one*. Whatever principle a person identifies as their primary guide tends to be the first they consider in any situation. If people don't view the golden rule as their main principle, they're less likely to even consider it in a given scenario and, as a result, less likely to act consistently with it. I believe the golden rule is often overlooked because many assume their primary principle must be more "sophisticated" or "complex". As mentioned earlier, the golden rule's simplicity is actually a strength. It provides clear and straightforward guidance on what to do.

To make our relationships more satisfying, we should encourage those around us to be more honest with themselves and better manage their impulses. We should also encourage them to recognize the primacy of the golden rule among their guiding principles.

EACH PERSON HAS IMPROVED THEIR RELATIONSHIP WITH THEMSELVES

Each person has two types of relationships: those with others and the one with themselves. When thinking about which relationships to improve in our lives, we often focus on others and overlook the one with ourselves. To "improve" this relationship means making it more emotionally satisfying.

Our emotional satisfaction with ourselves is deeply shaped by the mental frameworks we rely on. To strengthen this connection and make it more fundamentally enjoyable, we must dismantle thought patterns that limit gratification and cause pain. Doing so makes it easier to enter the playful mind and increase happiness. Without these efforts, our enjoyment remains limited and our pain is greater.

When people try to improve their bonds with others, they often focus only on the external dynamic. What they often overlook is that the quality of those bonds is deeply influenced by the quality of their relationship with themselves. When our connection with ourselves is unsatisfying, our relationships with others tend to suffer too. Blocked inner enjoyment and increased emotional pain affect how we interact with others. Preoccupied with these thoughts and feelings, it becomes harder to enter the playful mind and fully engage in shared moments. Sometimes, we may even lash out at others. Internal suffering inevitably spills over into our relationships.

A satisfying connection with ourselves lays the foundation for deeply fulfilling bonds with others. As our enjoyment becomes less inhibited and our pain decreases, our interactions with others are increasingly guided by inner happiness. Being more at peace and relaxed makes it easier to cultivate the playful mind and engage in the time we share with others. We are also less likely to lash out at people.

Given this, I would say that our *internal* connection "caps" the satisfaction we can gain from our external relationships. We can only deepen our bond with another person so much before further growth requires first strengthening our relationship with ourselves. When blocked enjoyment and anguish exist within, there's a limit to how much fulfillment our external connections can provide.

Our bond with another becomes more enjoyable when both of us have strengthened our connections with ourselves. When considering a connection with someone else, there are always three relationships to keep in mind: one external and two internal. When either or both internal connections improve, the external one improves as well. Conversely, when either or both internal connections deteriorate, the external bond suffers too.

How We Can Help Each Other Improve Our Internal Connections

The more we develop a fundamental understanding of ourselves, the more our connection with ourselves improves and becomes satisfying. Without moving toward this self-awareness, this relationship remains stagnant.

But no one has to rely solely on themselves to reach this understanding. We can support each other in the process. This includes helping one another unlearn mental frameworks that block enjoyment and cause distress, as well as refining our models of reality. We can also assist in removing obstacles that interfere with cultivating the playful mind. By doing so, we help each other strengthen our internal relationships.

When we care about someone, the desire to help them improve their internal connection can be very strong. In these cases, the most important relationship to us isn't the external one we share with them, but their relationship with themselves. While we understand that improving their internal connection will also benefit our external bond, those benefits are incidental. They aren't the primary reason we want to help. Above all, we simply don't want to see the people we care about suffer. We want to see them happy.

How Our Relationship With Ourselves Evolves

Our connection with ourselves evolves through two distinct stages:

Stage #1: We recognize that our pain and blocked gratification stem from the mental frameworks we apply and from not having sufficiently developed our model of reality.

Stage #2: We disassemble these mental frameworks and build out our picture of reality in enough detail.

As our relationship with ourselves progresses through these two stages, it shifts from emotional suffering and blocked contentment toward genuine satisfaction. There are five "emotional transitions" worth noting:

- Moving away from a lack of happiness to more consistent happiness by developing a more playful mind. This more open mental state helps us engage with the present and enrich that happiness with other enjoyable emotions.
- Moving toward greater feelings of clarity and empowerment as we better grasp the foundational building blocks of our reality.
- Moving away from low self-esteem to more easily finding our innate self-value. We have unlearned the belief that we are fundamentally worthless.
- Moving away from self-hatred to inner peace. This self-hatred stems largely from us acting inconsistently with our own conscience. When we recognize how to be more honest about what is in our conscience and how to manage our impulses, this self-hatred can be replaced with peace.
- Moving away from despair to optimism. We do this by dismantling happiness conditions and expanding the range of outcomes we can feel optimistic about beyond just the final one.

The end result of improving our connection with ourselves is a more "integrated self". This self's components no longer conflict or battle each other but instead work together in peace and harmony. It may have been difficult for parts of the self to accept and collaborate when we first recognized that some aspects were limiting our gratification or causing harm. For example, we might feel hostile toward the ego because we see how its desire for power can deteriorate our emotional state. We may view this part as a "threat" or an "enemy that must be destroyed".

By dismantling the ego's attachment to power, we allow a new, less harmful version of the ego to emerge. One far less likely to cause suffering. After this transformation, we no longer see the ego as a "threat" or "enemy", but can accept and integrate this new version into the self.

We can foster a greater sense of integration by recognizing that every part of us is on the "same team", working together toward the shared goal of happiness. With this mindset, when we identify a part of ourselves that blocks enjoyment or causes pain, we seek to understand what drives it rather than hate it. Adopting this collaborative perspective improves our chances of recognizing harmful mental frameworks and figuring out how to discard them.

When We Don't Address Our Own Issues, We Unfairly Expect Our Relationships to Fix Them

As mentioned, when we neglect our internal relationship, our satisfaction is limited, we suffer more, and struggle to feel genuine happiness. As a result, we may become reliant on external sources to solve our emotional problems and bring us happiness. One such external source we can become dependent on is our romantic relationships.

A romantic bond can add satisfaction and enhance the happiness we already have, but it can't fix pre-existing emotional issues or create happiness we don't yet possess. When we enter a relationship expecting it to do these things and it doesn't, we often blame the other person. We may then believe we're in the wrong relationship and decide to leave. What we may not realize is that no relationship could fully solve these underlying issues. If we really want to address our emotional issues and find happiness, we must improve our internal relationship with ourselves.

By letting go of the expectation that a romantic relationship can fix our pre-existing emotional problems and make us happy, we remove much unnecessary pressure from that bond. As a result, the connection becomes far more enjoyable.

A Deeper Look at Self-Esteem and Trust Issues

So far in this book, we have dismantled various harmful thought patterns that weaken our internal connection and, in turn, our external bonds with others. In the next section, we will explore specific *self-esteem* and *trust* issues that significantly contribute to this deterioration. We'll examine these issues separately, including strategies for dismantling them.

STOPPING OUR SELF-ESTEEM ISSUES FROM HURTING OUR RELATIONSHIPS

As discussed in Chapter 2, at the core of our self-esteem issues lies the belief that we are fundamentally worthless. This belief may have been conditioned into us from a young age and leads to feelings of inherent worthlessness.

In addition, we may have been conditioned to tie our self-value to reaching specific outcomes. Through this link, our ability to reach these goals becomes a measure of personal value in our minds. For example, we might base our self-worth on winning competitions or being right in arguments.

When we believe we have no fundamental value, we can become very *anxious* and *angry* when we don't attain the outcomes tied to our self-value. This explains why we often feel distressed when we're not winning or when our arguments are demonstrated to be wrong. We experience anxiety and anger because we fear losing the "mental protection" that shields us from our self-perception of inherent worthlessness.

In situations where we don't attain these outcomes, another person is often involved. For example, we may not be winning a game because the other person is, or they may have pointed out a contradiction in our argument. In such cases, we often direct our anxiety and anger toward them, *seeing them as the cause* of the emotional pain we're experiencing — the pain rooted in our sense of inherent worthlessness. When our interactions with others are filled with anxiety and anger, the relationship suffers as well.

Ironically, the cause of our feeling inherently worthless is not the other person, but our own belief that we lack fundamental value. This belief also fuels the anxiety and anger we may direct toward others. It adversely affects both our internal relationship with ourselves and our external relationships with others. In my view, people with significant self-esteem issues often experience high levels of anxiety and anger in their external relationships. These tend to go hand in hand.

We can remove anxiety and anger from our interactions and relationships by dismantling the belief that we are fundamentally worthless. When we undo this belief, the corresponding emotions disappear as well. Afterward, we detach our personal value from goals like winning or being right. Our ability to meet these objectives will no longer be measures of our personal value. With no inherent worthlessness to shield against, it becomes easier to recognize the innate self-esteem that was always present but hard to "hear". This natural sense of self-worth should be enough for us. We shouldn't feel the need to reinforce it by tying our value to objectives.

By doing this, we should no longer feel anxious or angry toward others when we don't attain the outcomes we desire. Moving forward, if we still pursue winning or having our arguments be right, it won't be out of a need for a mental shield or self-esteem issues. Instead, we will pursue them because we genuinely find these experiences emotionally enjoyable.

Believing we're inherently worthless can drive anxiety and anger in our relationships, but *who we blame* often depends on the objectives we've tied our personal value to. We will now take a closer look at the four most common types of outcomes people tie their self-value to, including winning and being right in arguments. By doing this, we can more easily recognize when either we or the person we're interacting with is channeling anxiety and anger caused by low self-esteem.

Outcome #1: Winning

Whether we believe we are fundamentally worthless and have tied our personal value to winning becomes evident in competitive activities. While playing tennis, if we start to lose, anxiety and anger arise as our feelings of inherent worthlessness surface. If we end up losing, those feelings are fully exposed. But even if we win, the relationship with the other person may still be unsatisfying. While we might not direct anxiety and anger at them, we could treat them without respect because we've mentally linked "winning" to a person's "worth".

By contrast, imagine the person we're playing tennis against doesn't believe they are fundamentally worthless and has only *lightly* tied their self-worth to winning. This person doesn't get anxious or angry when they think they're losing because they aren't relying on winning to shield themselves from feelings of worthlessness. If they do lose, they don't suffer emotionally. If they win, they continue to treat us with the same respect as before. They don't see our intrinsic value as affected by the outcome. Overall, they don't direct anxiety, anger, or disrespect toward us.

When we believe we are fundamentally worthless and tie our personal value to winning, we may become paranoid and view everything we engage in as a competition with winners and losers. This can lead us to treat activities that aren't inherently competitive as if they are. For example, we might see a simple conversation as a contest to determine who tells the "better" story. Constantly — and unnecessarily — framing interactions this way only increases the anxiety and anger we direct toward others.

A key issue with relying on winning to mentally shield us from impaired self-esteem is that it's not a "stable" shield. Even when we win at tennis, it's only in one sport, in one arena, at one moment in time. We haven't won in every other sport, nor in the many non-sport contests like chess, debating, and so on. We might even lose the next time we play tennis. Winning once doesn't mean we've won at everything, everywhere, for all the time. This is why, even after a victory, we can still feel anxious and angry toward other people in future competitions.

The only way to break free from this cycle is to stop believing we are fundamentally worthless and to detach our personal value from winning. Once we do, our interactions and relationships become much more enjoyable.

Outcome #2: Being Right in Arguments

Whether we believe we are fundamentally worthless and have tied our personal value to being right can often be seen in our conversations with others.

When someone points out a flaw in what we're saying, we can become anxious and angry because it directly exposes our impaired self-esteem. Again, this anxiety and anger are often directed at the other person. We tend to interpret challenges to our argument as attacks on our sense of worth, seeing them as "personal attacks". However, it's not the other person who causes this emotional distress. It stems from our pre-existing belief that we are fundamentally worthless. We end up blaming others, even though we are the ones inflicting this distress on ourselves.

By contrast, imagine the other person does not believe they are fundamentally worthless and has not tied their personal value to being right. If we challenge their arguments, they wouldn't feel worthless. They can have their arguments questioned without seeing it as an attack on their self-worth or as a personal attack. They won't respond with anxiety or anger toward us. If we want to make our conversations and relationships with others more enjoyable, we need to stop believing we are fundamentally worthless and stop tying our self-worth to being right.

People who tie their self-esteem to being right often struggle to be honest with themselves when they've made a genuine error. They find it difficult to admit they're wrong because doing so requires mental fortitude to face both destabilizing feelings and low self-esteem. The combined emotional discomfort is a lot more overwhelming, so they often pretend the error doesn't exist.

A person's inability to admit they're wrong can make a relationship frustrating. Their conversations don't really go anywhere. To help them be more honest with themselves about mistakes, they need to untether their self-worth from being right. Self-honesty becomes easier because then they only have to face the destabilizing feelings — not the added burden of low self-esteem.

Outcome #3: Whether Other People Care About Us

When we believe we are inherently worthless and tie our self-value to whether others care, we often direct anxiety and anger toward those we perceive as not caring in the way we'd like.

When we believe someone cares about us, we feel shielded from our deep feelings of worthlessness, though they haven't disappeared. When we think someone doesn't care, that shield is gone, exposing us to the emotional pain we've been trying to hide. This leads to anxiety and anger directed at that person, whom we see as the cause of our distress. Again, it's our own belief in our lack of fundamental worth that is the actual cause.

By contrast, a person who feels inherently worthy and hasn't tied their self-value to others' care is unlikely to respond with anger or anxiety when that care seems lacking.

We tend to tie our personal value more closely to whether people show romantic interest in us. As a result, we are more prone to anxiety and anger in romantic relationships than in familial or platonic ones. Our self-worth may become so linked to romantic affection that we become paranoid they don't genuinely value us, sometimes misinterpreting their behavior as signs of indifference when they actually do.

Overall, our relationships with others become much more satisfying and enjoyable when we unlearn the belief that we are fundamentally worthless and stop tying our personal value to others' attention. Without doing this, it can become difficult to ever relax in our external connections.

Outcome #4: Being in a Romantic Relationship

When we believe we are fundamentally worthless and tie our self-worth to being in a romantic relationship, we often direct anxiety and anger toward our partner when we think they might leave.

We may find it hard to exit a relationship where the other person repeatedly acts immorally because we rely on it to protect us from feeling low self-esteem. Once we stop believing we are inherently worthless and detach our personal value, it becomes easier to walk away from such a relationship.

STOPPING OUR TRUST ISSUES FROM HURTING OUR RELATIONSHIPS

Our ability to trust someone not to do us wrong is clearly crucial for a satisfying relationship. When someone close lets us down, we not only lose trust in them but may also find it harder to trust others in the future. So, how can we rebuild our capacity to trust people?

Find a More Reliable Basis for Trusting Someone

If we want to find people more likely to act consistently with their conscience, we should seek those with high mental fortitude. As discussed, such individuals are more honest when their stated principles don't align with their deeper values and are more willing to acknowledge their capacity to act immorally. Consequently, they are more likely to take active steps to manage these impulses and hold themselves accountable when they do wrong.

People with low mental fortitude and self-deceptive tendencies tend to be less trustworthy. They are more likely to deceive themselves when they notice a mismatch between their stated principles and their moral compass. They will deny having urges to act immorally, and so will not manage them. Even if made to recognize that their behavior is ordinarily unethical, they will convince themselves they have a special justification that makes it acceptable.

With this approach, we will hopefully strike a better balance of trusting the correct people while still recognizing who the wrong people are to trust.

Let Go of Needing to Be 100% Certain Someone Is Trustworthy

After a betrayal, we might be willing to trust others, but only if we're 100% certain they won't wrong us. We need to relax this standard at least a little, or we'll never find anyone to trust. After all, what we primarily rely on to judge someone's moral integrity is their words and actions. All we can do is form a belief about the likelihood they'll act ethically or unethically. And it will always be just a likelihood.

If we accept that 100% certainty is impossible, then our next best option is to find people who, based on our observations, have a higher likelihood of acting ethically. In my view, these are people who most demonstrate qualities of high mental fortitude and self-honesty.

Stop the Ego from Caring About Looking Foolish for Trusting the Wrong Person Again

In my view, the desire to trust only those we're 100% certain about after a betrayal ultimately comes from the ego. It felt foolish and painful to trust the wrong person before and it has a strong desire to not feel that way again.

If we want to let go of the strong desire to trust only those we're absolutely certain about, we need to challenge our ego's fear of looking silly for trusting the incorrect person again. The way to do this is by again helping the ego recognize that this way of thinking actually makes it the greater fool.

As mentioned, if we only trust people we are 100% certain about, we will end up trusting no one. While this may protect us from betrayal by someone close, it also means we won't have anyone close at all. In doing so, we miss out on all the satisfying experiences that come from trusting the right people. We lose the richness, nuance, and depth that close connections bring.

Our ability to trust others is one of the most courageous and valuable qualities we can experience. We shouldn't give it up without a fight. A person can hurt us and waste our time, but losing this ability means losing something truly sacred. Ultimately, it's up to us whether we give it up, not them.

It is a greater folly to forgo these enjoyable experiences with others and ourselves out of fear of looking foolish; especially when the harm we hope to avoid is statistically unlikely. We sacrifice a wealth of satisfaction for something with only a small chance of occurring. Some people fear being fooled so much that they see this sacrifice as worthwhile. While I understand that response, I believe it is an even greater mistake.

Challenge the Notion That We Were Particularly Foolish for Misplacing Our Trust

When we trust someone, it's usually because, based on what we've observed of their behavior so far, they seem well-intentioned. Sometimes, it will turn out that our reading was correct and they are someone who does the right thing. Other times, our reading will be incorrect and they end up doing the wrong thing.

At the end of the day, it all comes down to *luck*. Yes, we can increase the chances of trusting the right person by identifying key qualities that suggest they're more likely to do the right thing. But ultimately, luck determines how things turn out. So, for those who tend to trust the right people more often, I don't think it's because they're experts at reading human behavior. It could be that they are a little bit better than most, but I think it's usually luck that the people they've trusted turn out to be the right ones.

I really see this like going to a casino. We all play the same odds. Some of us leave with money; others don't. Sure, some people win more because they have greater expertise. But for most who walk away with money, it's mostly luck, not skill, that got them there. I mention this because no one should feel more foolish than others for trusting someone they shouldn't. Nor should anyone believe they have a special deficiency in reading others when this happens. They likely have the same ability as most, including those who generally trust the right people.

When Is It Okay to Trust Someone Again After They've Betrayed Our Trust?

I think it's acceptable to trust this person again, provided they have since developed the qualities that make someone more likely to do what is right. These are the questions we should be asking ourselves:

- Do they have the mental fortitude to be honest with themselves about their capacity to do wrong, or do they deceive themselves?
- Have they managed their impulses sufficiently?

If the answers to all these questions are "yes", then I believe we can trust this person again. If any answer is "no", they are likely to repeat the same action if given the chance. To find out, we need to talk openly with the person and, after these conversations, honestly assess whether we believe their responses. I'd be very wary of anyone who's only sorry because they got caught, not because they've sincerely accepted that what they did was wrong.

To form this view of whether someone has developed the qualities that make them more likely to do what is right, we still rely on our interpretation of what they say and do. So, we can never be completely certain. At best, we can believe they have a higher likelihood of acting rightly. Ultimately, it can be difficult to tell if someone has genuinely changed until we observe how they behave when their impulses are tested.

HOW A PERSON UNLOCKS THESE VITAL TRAITS WITHIN THEMSELVES

A person unlocks the traits vital to a satisfying relationship by having enough mental fortitude to be honest with themselves. Only with this mental strength can they understand themselves well enough to recognize the importance of these traits and work to develop them.

Without such self-honesty, a person will struggle to identify what needs to change within themselves for their connections to improve.

With greater self-honesty, we should recognize not only that our emotional suffering is often caused by our mental frameworks, but also that we are *primarily responsible* for managing our own mental and emotional states. If we feel anger, we should seek to understand what in our thinking is driving it, rather than blaming the other person and assuming they're the main reason. If we do lash out, we should apologize and work harder to understand how to change ourselves.

People who lack this self-honesty are less likely to acknowledge this responsibility over their own state of mind. They are more likely to blame others for their feelings, lash out, and refuse to apologize. They are unlikely to really commit to bettering themselves. Improving our relationship with ourselves is important not just from a practical standpoint, but an ethical one too.

Ultimately, to increase contentment in our bonds, we should encourage those around us to develop this mental strength and capacity for self-honesty. Arguably, this is the most important trait we must possess to make our relationships as enjoyable as possible.

11

TRIGGERING SPECIFIC FEELINGS TO ENHANCE OUR HAPPINESS

All the previous chapters have focused on removing what disrupts our ability to enter the playful mind. This involves breaking down mental frameworks that block gratification and cause pain, as well as sufficiently completing our model of reality.

By entering the playful mind, we become receptive to engaging with each moment as it arises. Since we can better engage with what we're presently doing, we can experience a fuller range of enjoyable emotions from it. These feelings enhance the happiness we already have simply by being in the playful mind. Each combination of feelings created in every moment of doing something is unique. Every moment of progression through an activity offers a different mix of sensations, emotions, and thoughts to interact with.

When we can more easily enter the playful mind, we should find that we can enjoy a much broader range of pursuits. Almost all activities should become a lot more satisfying, even those we might ordinarily think of as mundane. After all, we now have a mindset that allows us to engage with the specific sensorial, emotional, and conceptual details that emerge in each moment of a task.

There are times when we want to enhance our happiness with a *specific satisfying emotion.* In these instances, it's useful to be aware of which activities are likely to trigger it. The last chapter of this book will focus on how to identify the triggers for the *basic categories of satisfaction.*

Before we go further into this, there are two things to note.

The first is that by intentionally choosing activities to evoke a specific satisfying feeling, we are "curating our emotional experience" in those moments. By contrast, when we select activities without a particular feeling in mind, we aren't curating our emotional experience. However, this lack of curation doesn't stop us from being mentally open to the pursuit or from accessing a wider range of enjoyable emotions during it.

For example, we might go for a walk without a specific goal in mind, simply enjoying the sights and sounds around us. Even without planning what to feel, we can still experience a variety of pleasant emotions like calm, curiosity, and joy. I mention this because I don't want anyone to think they must curate their emotional experiences every moment to feel satisfied. We can still feel satisfied even if we don't.

The second point is that it's not always easy to say some endeavors provide "better" or "more satisfying" feelings than others. As discussed back in Chapter 1, I've found that, more often than not, endeavors aren't necessarily "more satisfying" than each other but offer similar levels of satisfaction in different ways. Some are like apples and oranges; they provide different combinations of enjoyable emotions that can't be easily compared. I mention this so we can focus more on appreciating the satisfaction we have, rather than measuring it against ideas of what is "best" or "better".

HOW THE ACTIVITY'S ELEMENTS "WORK TOGETHER" TO CREATE SATISFACTION

The mix of enjoyable emotions we experience at any moment during a task depends on exactly what we're doing at that time. As a result, this mix can change from one moment to the next as the activity itself changes. This means that within a single task, we can create different combinations of gratifying emotions across its many moments — not just repeat the same combination over and over.

To be more precise, the specific mix of enjoyable emotions we experience at any given moment depends on how the *elements* of the activity "work together" at that point in time. The gratification we get from a moment arises from the *interactions and dynamics* between these elements at that stage. Let's explore some examples of actions to better understand this causal relationship.

Drink Tomato Soup

The elements would be the ingredients of a soup, which include chopped onion, olive oil, vegetable broth, tomatoes, basil, salt, and pepper.

In each moment of drinking the soup, we're tasting not just the individual ingredients, but how they play off each other. The specific way these ingredients come together in that instant, flavor-wise, is the interaction and dynamic between them. This is also what creates the satisfying feeling at that moment.

Each moment of drinking the soup is different because the balance of ingredients in each mouthful always varies. Sometimes there's more chopped onion and less salt; other times, less chopped onion and more basil. As the balance shifts, so do the interactions and dynamics we taste, which changes the satisfying feeling we experience.

Listen to a Song

The elements are the instruments used in the song which include lead guitar, bass guitar, keyboard, and drums.

In each moment of listening to this song, we hear not just the notes played by each instrument, but how they blend together. The particular way these notes combine at that instant, in terms of sound, is the interaction and dynamic between them. Again, this is where the satisfying feeling comes from at that point in time.

Each moment of listening to this song is different because the notes played by each instrument are constantly changing. As the notes change, so do the musical relationships we hear. This, in turn, affects the satisfying feeling we experience as the song unfolds.

Watch a Play

The elements are everything that makes up this play, including the stage sets and actors.

In each moment of watching a play, we see not just the stage sets and actors, but how they work together. This includes not only how the actors physically interact with the stage sets but also how they engage with each other through conversation and behavior. Again, the particular way they come together in each instant — the interaction and dynamic between these elements — is where the satisfying feeling emerges.

Each moment of watching a play is different because the interactions and flow between the actors and the stage sets are constantly shifting. Again, this changes the emotional tones we experience as the play progresses.

The Challenge of Predicting Which Interactions and Dynamics Will Emerge

If we want an activity to produce specific emotions, we need to include elements that interact in ways that generate them. Figuring out this puzzle of which elements to combine can be fun.

It can be quite difficult though to predict the interplay that will emerge when we put various elements together. What actually manifests might differ greatly from our expectations. It could be less satisfying, more satisfying, or equally satisfying, but in a way different from what we were seeking. This challenge in creating the feeling we want becomes clearer when revisiting the examples above:

- We put specific ingredients in a tomato soup expecting a particular taste, but it turns out differently than expected.
- We combine specific notes in a song expecting a specific sound, but the result is quite different from what we predicted.
- We bring specific actors together in a scene expecting a distinct chemistry, but their interaction doesn't match our expectations.

We can often predict the general interactions and dynamics that will emerge, but *predicting their details* is much harder. Once again, we can see how challenging this is by revisiting the examples above:

- The ingredients in a tomato soup may taste broadly as expected, but the details of the flavor may differ.
- The notes in a song may create the general sound we intended, but the specifics often vary.
- The actors in a play may have the chemistry we envisioned overall, but the nuances often don't match our expectations exactly.

The Challenge of Predicting Which Emotions Will Emerge

Since the detailed interactions and dynamics are difficult to predict, so too are the resulting emotions we feel. We can often anticipate the general feeling but not its finer details. For example, if directing a film, we might expect that adding particular elements to a scene will evoke a general sense of excitement, but it's hard to predict its exact quality. Excitement can take many forms. Given this, it's easier to "engineer" a broad feeling into an activity than to create something highly specific and nuanced. Still doable, but harder.

I don't think it's ever really possible for us to imagine every detail of a satisfying feeling before we experience it. We might envision it broadly, with some specifics, but not all. Even after experiencing it, recalling every detail is difficult. We can remember the general feelings of tasting soup, listening to a song, or watching a play, but not all the nuances. To me, this invites us to experience those elements and their interplay again.

This difficulty in predicting what feelings will emerge when elements come together is one reason I have a lot of respect for serious creatives. I consider myself only mildly creative by comparison. I admire their ability to take risks in combining elements, fully aware there's no guarantee the resulting feeling will match their vision. The emotional effect only becomes clear upon execution. And even then, they can't predict whether everyone will respond the same way.

The Challenge With Noticing These Interactions and Dynamics

When we have a playful mind *engaged* with an activity, we can notice these interactions and dynamics and draw satisfaction from them. When interference disrupts this mindset, sustaining our connection to the task becomes much harder. Without engagement, we either overlook the patterns and relationships and gain no satisfaction, or we notice them but still feel no gratification. This is why it's vital to cultivate a mind that is receptive to what we do.

HOW TO TRIGGER *BASIC* SATISFYING FEELINGS

We cultivate these basic types of satisfaction by "adjusting" the elements of an activity in four ways. Another way to think about it is that there are four "levers" we can manipulate in almost everything we do to trigger these core forms of enjoyment.

Lever #1: Increase or Decrease the Number of Elements in the Activity

When an activity involves fewer elements, the interactions and dynamics tend to create emotional tones of *simplicity* and *tranquility*.

These feelings can be quite satisfying when we're in the mood for them.

When there are a larger number of elements, the interplay that emerges can be quite complex. If these elements interact in an "ordered way", they can create emotional tones of *elegance* and *grace*. If they interact in a "disordered way", the tone may be one of *chaos*. Whether we find these feelings of elegance or chaos satisfying depends again on what we're in the mood for.

The more elements there are in an activity, the more difficult it generally becomes to have them interact in an ordered way. For this reason, each additional element makes it harder to create a tone of elegance — and increases the likelihood of creating a tone of chaos. That said, if we can successfully bring order to a larger group of elements, we can create a feeling of elegance that is likely to be highly satisfying.

To be clear, the interplay among a greater number of elements isn't necessarily more enjoyable than that among fewer elements. It really depends on our mood. Sometimes, we might prefer simplicity over elegance or chaos. In addition, the interplay from a small number of elements, while simple, can still be rich, deep, and nuanced. Whether it's two instruments playing off each other or two actors working a scene, the enjoyment can be quite layered. The range and depth of these dynamics depend on how complementary the elements are. Some elements may not complement each other well, resulting in a more limited range and depth.

Lever #2: Increase or Decrease How Active We Are in the Activity

We are also an element within any activity we take part in. The interactions and dynamics we experience with other elements influence our enjoyment.

As a participant, there's a spectrum of how "active" we are. In activities where we are "more active", we must take action to keep things moving; such as when playing a musical instrument or acting in a TV show. In activities where we are "less active", they progress without our input, like when we listen to a song or watch a movie.

When we are more active, there is a greater feeling of *involvement* and *responsibility*. When we are less active, we feel more detached and less responsible. Whether these feelings are satisfying or not depends again on our disposition at that point in time. Neither experience is inherently better or worse than the other.

Lever #3: Increase or Decrease the Number of Elements That Are Reactive to Us in the Activity

When we do something where we are "active" on some level, there is also a degree to how "reactive" the other elements are to us. That is, how much their behavior shifts in response to ours. For example:

- If we are playing in a jazz band, the other musicians may change their notes or energy in response to what we play and the vibe we bring.
- If we are acting in a TV show, our performance can influence the reactions of fellow actors in the scene. While we can't change the dialogue, the emotion we bring can affect their delivery.
- If we are playing tennis, our opponent constantly reacts and repositions themselves based on where we hit the ball.

For elements to be "less reactive" to us, their behavior during the activity does not change in response to ours. For example:

- If we are listening to a prerecorded song, the music does not respond to our actions.
- If we are watching a TV show, the content remains unchanged regardless of how we behave.
- If we are watching tennis — whether live or on TV — the game is largely unaffected by what we do.

When engaging in something more reactive, we feel more *connected* to the world around us, as if part of a living, breathing ecosystem. When it's less reactive, we do not feel as connected. Neither experience is inherently more enjoyable than the other. Again, it depends on our disposition at the time.

Lever #4: Increase or Decrease the Familiarity of the Element Combinations in the Activity

The more familiar we are with a combination of elements, the more acquainted we become with the interplay it creates. Experiencing such familiar patterns can be comforting and reassuring when that's what we're in the mood for. Conversely, unfamiliar combinations produce new and unexpected interactions. Experiencing these unfamiliar patterns can evoke feelings of *discovery* and the *sublime*.

This feeling of discovery can arise even when interacting with a combination of elements we're well acquainted with. While many patterns within that combination may be familiar, it can still reveal dynamics that have remained *hidden* until now. Hidden depth and range can emerge not only in our interactions with others but also when playing a musical instrument or a sport. For example, a fixed set of piano keys offers numerous permutations of sound, and playing a sport involves many subtle levels of strategy. Something familiar in one sense can simultaneously feel unfamiliar in another, producing both comfort and reassurance alongside a sense of discovery.

Another way to create a feeling of discovery with a familiar combination of elements is by introducing an additional element. This new element might be entirely unfamiliar to us, or it could be something we've encountered before but never seen interact with the current elements. Once again, the activity can feel both familiar in one way and unfamiliar in another.

To preserve the emotional tone of discovery throughout an experience, we should avoid learning everything about its elements beforehand. We should learn just enough to get started, but if we learn too much upfront, we risk losing that feeling. For example, when playing a video game, many of us use guides that walk us through every section to avoid missing items, quests, weapons, and more. While this helps us complete the game 100%, it also diminishes the feeling of discovery because we are aware of everything that is about to happen. Ironically, in our fear of missing out, we end up missing one of the most enjoyable feelings we can experience. Part of the fun is figuring out this *hidden interplay* ourselves.

Sometimes our *expectations* can hold us back from discovering new interactions and dynamics. When we combine elements, we often have specific patterns in mind that we want or expect to emerge. We select elements we believe are more likely to produce those desired outcomes and avoid others. Sometimes we never even try mixing particular elements because we expect the result won't be rewarding — despite never having tested that combination. In this way, our expectations can limit us from uncovering genuinely interesting and satisfying relationships. That's why I believe it's valuable to sometimes add elements without any expectation of what interplay will arise. This openness can also be quite fun.

Each of These Levers Can Be Manipulated by Degrees

When manipulating these levers in an activity, we can adjust them to varying degrees. For example, we could *radically, moderately, or subtly* increase or decrease:

- The number of elements.
- How active we are.
- How reactive the other elements are to us.
- How familiar the combination of elements is.

Radical, moderate, or subtle manipulation of these levers leads to shifts in the interactions and dynamics between the elements. These shifts, in turn, affect the degree to which the enjoyable emotions change. For example:

- A radical decrease in the number of elements can shift the satisfying feeling from chaos to simplicity.
- A subtle decrease in the familiarity of the combination of elements can lead to a slight reduction in comfort and assurance.

These shifts in enjoyable emotions can be seen as "tonal shifts" within the activity. Even when we're not actively manipulating the levers, the elements are constantly rearranging themselves around us — at least in subtle ways. This means there are always subtle tonal shifts happening in each moment. We might not always notice them, but they're there. Sometimes, the elements rearrange in more moderate or even radical ways, leading to corresponding moderate and radical tonal shifts.

Other Levers We Can Manipulate in Our Activities

Most activities include levers we can adjust to influence our enjoyment. The four we've discussed are among the most common. In addition to these, there are also more "specialized levers" that apply only to specific activities or groups of similar activities. For example, in filmmaking, such niche levers include lighting, directing actors, composing shots, and so on.

Manipulating these niche levers can create unique and nuanced enjoyable emotions. For example, the excitement generated in a film scene can feel very different from that experienced while performing live in a band, because the specialized levers involved in each are so distinct.

Typically, both common and specialized levers are present in everything we do. Clearly, it would be impossible to document every one across all domains. That said, many books have explored these controls in depth by focusing on specific fields or practices. I think the beauty of doing anything lies in our own personal exploration of these levers. They are initially hidden, waiting to be discovered.

What Ultimately Determines Which Interactions and Dynamics "Work" for Us and Which Do Not?

Ultimately, it is our brain that determines this. We will never fully understand why our brain registers particular interactions and dynamics as working in a way that is satisfying for us. It just does. Likewise, we will also never fully grasp why our brain registers other interplay as "not working" and being less enjoyable.

When we come across something that is working on *multiple levels in such a uniform and complementary way*, we consider it to be "well-crafted". Sometimes the activity as a whole is not well-crafted, but a particular moment or moments are. A film that overall isn't great may still have some standout sequences. It's in these instances that we can feel awe at how well they've been put together. This is a very gratifying feeling.

HOW TO CULTIVATE DEEPER ENGAGEMENT WITH AN ACTIVITY

When we're "deeply engaged" in something, we become *more attentive* to its elements, interactions, and dynamics. This heightened attention allows us to produce a broader range of enjoyable emotions while doing it.

Find the Interesting Angle

To reach this level of engagement, we simply need to find the activity *interesting* in some way. Most things offer at least one angle we can genuinely connect with. It doesn't have to capture everyone's attention — only ours. What we find interesting always relates to the sensations, emotions, or ideas it evokes.

Find the Challenge

To *further deepen* our absorption, it helps to find challenges in what we're doing. This requires aiming for a desirable outcome that has some degree of difficulty. It doesn't have to be extremely hard, just hard enough. In moments where there's a strong risk of not getting the outcome due to that difficulty, our engagement tends to intensify.

Our thoughts become *consumed* with solving the puzzle of how to overcome obstacles and reach the intended result. This deepened engagement brings a strong, satisfying feeling of drive. Our immersion grows even more when we find the challenge interesting and fun. I'm not especially skilled at playing my synths, but I enjoy the challenge of improvising something that — even if not "good" — still works on some level.

We can set *multiple* challenges within a task by aiming for several desirable outcomes. For example, in a game of squash, we might aim not only to win but also to pull off at least two trick shots. Obstacles can also be tied to specific phases of a task. For instance, making a film involves development, production, and distribution, with each phase presenting its own set of hurdles.

Impose Constraints on Ourselves

We can also create challenges within a task by choosing *constraints* to impose on ourselves. For example, when playing squash, we might choose to use only backhand shots and avoid forehands entirely. These self-imposed limits can be fun and may even lead to the discovery or creation of new styles of play. It can be exciting to see how far we can go — to explore what's possible — within those constraints.

When we're constrained in our creative endeavors, such as making music, we often have to think outside the box to work within the limitation. This can lead us to create things we never would have imagined without the constraint. Whether voluntary or involuntary, constraints often lead to innovation. That's why they're often accompanied by a strong sense of discovery.

What can make it difficult to pursue challenges is the ego, which may fear looking foolish for believing we can overcome them. In this way, the ego becomes an obstacle to deeper engagement with our tasks. As discussed in Chapter 8, we can quiet the ego's concerns by recognizing that this fear reflects the mindset of the "greater fool". That is, we avoid challenges to protect ourselves from appearing silly. Yet in doing so, we give up access to a wide range of enjoyable emotions. It's not a worthwhile trade.

Find Peace in the Tension

One thing we can do when deeply engaging with an activity is to "find peace in the tension". This can be a very satisfying experience.

This tension is created in moments where there's a strong risk of not reaching a desired outcome. For example, if we aim to win a game of squash, the tension is created and sustained for as long as there's a strong possibility of losing. It rises and falls in proportion to that risk. When we're far ahead, the risk is low and the tension decreases. But when we're behind by a few points — or neck and neck — the pressure intensifies.

When finding peace in the tension, we are not eliminating the tension itself. Instead, we create a feeling of peace within our center and let the pressure move to the background or the edges of our awareness. The tension is still there — it surrounds us — but it no longer occupies our center. It's a bit like being in the eye of a storm.

This inner peace often takes the form of a *peaceful rhythm* — something dynamic and alive, even if only subtly. In this mental state, I've found that I can think clearly, even while the pressure remains in the background. Once the task is over, the tension is fully released. Either I've attained the desired outcome, or I haven't.

This exercise can go by these other names:

- Finding order in the chaos.

- Finding harmony in the disharmony.
- Finding comfort in the discomfort.

Manage the Tension

Once we find peace in the tension, it becomes much easier to *manage*. When we encounter tension in a task due to the risk of not meeting our goal, our instinct is usually to reduce it. For example, in a game of squash, we might try to win points quickly to eliminate the pressure that comes from the possibility of losing. In this case, reducing the tension is one way of managing it.

However, we can also choose to *maintain* the tension — or even *increase* it. Why would we do this? It depends on the task, but managing the pressure in this way can be deeply gratifying. There's a unique satisfaction in becoming more comfortable with its presence. Rather than trying to eliminate it, we can learn to ride it. It's empowering to discover new ways of interacting with tension beyond simply trying to reduce it.

It becomes much easier to choose to maintain or increase the pressure once we've found peace within it. The "cycles of tension" come more under our control. We can choose to let it rise and fall multiple times throughout the task. We can also decide the degree to which the pressure rises and falls: subtle, moderate, or radical.

This *rise and fall* can be seen as our intentional increase and partial release of tension during the activity. As mentioned above, it's only at the end of the task that the pressure is fully released. Without finding peace in the tension, however, we're more likely to try to eliminate it as soon as it arises.

Healthy and Unhealthy Types of Tension

It's useful to be aware of these two types, as one should be sought and the other avoided.

We experience unhealthy tension during an activity when our desire for a particular outcome is driven by issues of self-esteem, ego, or happiness conditions. In moments where there's a risk of not attaining the intended result, we don't just feel the usual pressure. It becomes mixed with dissatisfying emotions such as:

- Fundamental worthlessness.
- Powerlessness, helplessness, and anger.
- Despair.

It's hard to find peace within unhealthy pressure, and therefore difficult to experience the satisfaction that comes from it. We also can't easily choose to maintain or increase this kind of pressure, so we miss out on that satisfying degree of control.

To make this tension less unhealthy, we need to discard the mental frameworks tied to self-worth, ego, and conditional happiness. Once these have been cleared away, we may still desire the same outcome from the activity, but that desire is no longer driven by those issues. The pressure that now arises from pursuing this goal, free from harmful thought patterns, is healthy.

The State of Surrender

As we deepen our engagement with an activity, we may reach a point where we enter a "state of surrender". From what I can tell, this is the deepest level of immersion we can experience.

While in this state of mind, our *full attention* is devoted to the elements, interactions, and dynamics unfolding in each moment of the activity. We're no longer consciously directing our thoughts; instead, they are being pulled and absorbed into the sensorial, emotional, and conceptual details of the experience. We don't reflect on ourselves — not even on how happy or satisfied we are — because our minds are too occupied with the doing. A state of surrender is a state of complete immersion. It's almost like being in a trance, being possessed, or under hypnosis.

Activities that more easily allow us to enter a state of surrender tend to have at least one of the following qualities.

First, there's usually a challenge we find genuinely interesting and fun. It doesn't have to be extremely difficult to draw us into a state of surrender; it just needs to be challenging enough.

Second, we're *highly active*, and the other elements are *highly reactive* to us, such as when playing a sport or dancing with another person. In these cases, there's an almost-immediate feedback loop: our action prompts their reaction, which prompts our next move, and so on. There's little time to consciously decide what to do next; we're forced to respond instinctively. Our thoughts aren't being deliberately directed. Instead, they're pulled along by the sensations and emotions arising in each moment. We're carried by them.

Third, we may simply have an "affinity" for the activity, something that's hard to explain. And I don't think we need to. Some of us are drawn to things that others aren't. One affinity I believe most of us share is listening to music. While our tastes differ, particular kinds of music can easily pull us into a state of surrender.

Frame Each Task as an "Act of Creation"

In each moment we are alive, we are engaged in some activity. This means that, at every point in time, various elements are coming together to form a specific combination of sensorial, emotional, and conceptual experiences. In this sense, each moment is an act of creation. The "creation" being this unique blend of sensations, emotions, and thoughts. Our mind is constantly interfacing with the creation of each moment.

When we frame the coming together of elements in each moment this way, the present actions become far more inviting for our mind to engage with. This is because the mind more clearly recognizes the activity as a source of nourishment and rejuvenation, experienced through sensations, emotions, and concepts.

With this framing, we should find our attention more drawn to the details of the present elements and their relationships. For example, if we frame a walk in the park as a creative act, our mind becomes more enticed to engage with the sound of leaves rustling in the wind, the smell of grass, and so on. It wants to more closely connect with the act of creation taking place.

Every act of creation holds a mysterious influence over us, as we can't fully grasp how the interaction of elements produces such an effect on the mind. We recognize that it moves us, even if we don't entirely understand how. Focusing on this mystery while enjoying its effect can deepen our immersion in the actions involved. Fortunately, we don't need to solve the mystery to enjoy the experience.

Once I recognized that there is an act of creation in each moment, it became difficult not to see every instant in that light. I believe this is because the framing touches on something fundamental about experience itself. It has since become a key lens through which I view each moment.

While in Deep Engagement, We Can Discover New Emotions

Some feelings can only arise through deep immersion, ranging from the subtle to the intense. When we encounter a new emotion, it can feel strange. Like discovering a hidden room in a house we've lived in our whole life.

If we're interested in mentally cataloging these new emotions, there's a hurdle. When we're deeply absorbed in what we're doing, our thoughts are so preoccupied with its elements, interactions, and dynamics that we rarely reflect on the satisfying emotions that emerge. Without that reflection, we can't register or retain those emotional tones. We're simply having too much fun.

That said, there are moments during deep immersion when we do notice these emotions, but they're rare. The more engrossed we are, the less often this reflection happens. Emotions experienced during states of surrender are the hardest to consciously register. To be clear, I don't think we need to catalog every emotion that arises. It's perfectly fine to just enjoy the experience without feeling a need to document or analyze it.

One of the enjoyable feelings we experience while engrossed is the "peaceful rhythm" we can find when there is tension. How this rhythm feels can vary between activities, and even between moments within the same activity. As the elements shift, the tension can change as well, which in turn alters the rhythm we encounter. These rhythms may feel similar at times, but they rarely feel exactly the same.

WARNINGS ABOUT DEEP ENGAGEMENT

We may feel as though we have to fully immerse ourselves in every activity that comes our way, as if we're not allowed to simply engage lightly or even disengage entirely at times.

We can feel this pressure because we believe we have to "make the most of life". To do that, we may think we need to be deeply engaged in every moment, or at least in as many of them as possible. While I do believe in making the most of life, constant deep engagement isn't the way to get there. Instead, we should aim for *sincere engagement* — giving our attention to things at the level we genuinely feel moved to in that moment.

If we strongly feel *averse* to deep engagement, it's better to either engage lightly or not engage at all. Forcing ourselves to immerse in something while feeling this resistance is unlikely to succeed, and unlikely to bring much gratification. That's because we're acting against what we genuinely feel inclined to do. In such moments, it's more satisfying to either interact with the task lightly or step away entirely.

That being said, we're not always good at predicting the elements, interactions, and dynamics that will unfold before we begin something. Sometimes we don't expect to engage deeply, but once we start, we find ourselves drawn in. In those cases, we sincerely want to continue with that level of immersion. That's why, even when I don't initially feel like doing something, I'll usually give it a try. If I end up fully engaged and genuinely want to keep going, I'll stick with it. If not, I'll either shift to light engagement or stop altogether.

The only time I won't give something a try is when, in that moment, I feel a strong aversion to it. Yes, I might be mistaken about how deeply I end up engaging with it. But when the reluctance is that intense, it's difficult to push myself to begin.

Sometimes we don't sincerely feel like doing something simply because we've done it a lot recently. Taking a break can give our sincere enthusiasm a chance to replenish.

Unpleasant Side Effects of Deep Engagement

While heavy immersion can seem highly desirable, there are two potential side effects worth being aware of.

The first side effect is mental fatigue. When we're drained in this way, we often don't feel like doing anything at all. The deeper the engagement, the more mentally taxing it can be. Fortunately, a good night's rest usually restores our energy, making it possible to immerse ourselves again the next day. Interestingly, while deep engagement can be exhausting, it can also refresh our outlook on life. It can be re-energizing on some level.

The second is the feeling of withdrawal. When we immerse ourselves deeply in an activity, it can create a chemical "high". This usually tapers off gradually, but when it ends abruptly, it can lead to this withdrawal. It can be unpleasant when it appears, but it eventually fades. The deeper the engagement, the greater the likelihood — and potential intensity — of withdrawal. States of surrender can be followed by a noticeable emotional dip, sometimes unpleasant enough to make us hesitant to seek deep immersion again.

While I don't think we can prevent withdrawal from arising, we can avoid responding to it in ways that make it worse. When we notice these feelings, it's important not to panic or become alarmed, as that can add layers of dissatisfaction. Sometimes we misinterpret withdrawal as a sign of a deeper mental issue, like depression — when in reality, it isn't. It's far better to acknowledge the feeling, ride it out, and let it pass.

INCREASING OUR MOTIVATION TO DO AN ACTIVITY

As discussed throughout the book, having a playful mind makes us more mentally open to engaging with what we do. However, being mentally receptive is not the same as being motivated to put in the effort.

Being mentally receptive means there isn't anything in our *philosophical outlook* preventing us from doing something. We're open to giving it a try and our philosophy may even encourage it. However, even with this openness, we may still lack the motivation to act, especially if the task seems effortful. Strong motivation is accompanied by an intense drive, whereas low motivation comes with a much weaker one.

Without strong motivation, we tend to stick to low-effort activities. These can still be satisfying, even leading to states of surrender; like when listening to music. However, by avoiding high-effort pursuits, we limit the variety of enjoyable emotions we experience. With stronger motivation, we're more likely to take on both easy and demanding tasks, expanding the emotional range that can enrich our happiness. So how can we increase our motivation to engage in high-effort activities?

Dismantle Demotivating Mental Frameworks

Breaking down the mental frameworks that block our enjoyment or cause us suffering also has the byproduct of strengthening our motivation.

When we dismantle thought patterns that limit our enjoyment, we expand the range of gratifying emotions we can draw from our actions. This makes effort feel more worthwhile, since there will be greater emotional rewards.

By dismantling thought patterns that cause distress, we avoid bringing unnecessary suffering into our activities. When suffering intrudes, it dampens enjoyment and weakens our drive to engage.

Reducing this baggage allows us to find more satisfaction in what we do, which in turn increases our motivation to apply ourselves.

Complete enough of our model of reality

By developing a sufficiently coherent picture of reality, we can focus more fully on our activities instead of being preoccupied with existential questions. When our desire to understand reality at a fundamental level goes unmet, it can be hard to feel motivated to do anything else. We may be driven to seek answers, but lack motivation for other pursuits.

Add Motivating Mental Frameworks

In the process of clarifying our picture of reality, we may develop mental frameworks that increase our motivation to expend effort. While this book explores several such frameworks, two key ones stand out.

The first is the belief that simply attempting something is likely to lead to fun, interesting, and engaging experiences. This belief motivates us to put in more effort because we're curious to see what experiences will emerge.

The second is the recognition that there is something fundamental about all our experiences that we will never fully understand. This sense of mystery creates a feeling of wonder, which can energize us and increase our motivation to strive harder.

Change Our Beliefs About What Drives Happiness

Our beliefs about what drives happiness can strongly influence how motivated we are to push ourselves. When we believe our happiness depends primarily on our activities, we're more likely to feel motivated to try harder. However, this motivation is often strongest at the beginning. As we try more things that fail to bring the happiness we hoped for, our drive to put in effort tends to fade.

When we recognize that happiness depends more on our internal state than on our activities, our motivation shifts. We become focused on learning how to reach the mental state that best supports happiness. Once we understand this and apply the necessary changes, it becomes easier to enter the playful mind. We begin to experience happiness without relying on any particular activity.

At that point, our motivation shifts once more. We're no longer driven to act in order to create happiness we lack, but to explore how we can deepen the happiness we already feel. We're curious about the enjoyable emotions that might arise when we engage with a task. We become inquisitive about the interplay that unfolds as we combine specific elements, and eager to discover the "levers" we can use to shape and influence them.

Shift Our Motivation to Be Driven More by the Carrot Than the Stick

When our motivation is driven by the stick, we act to avoid suffering. When it's driven by the carrot, we act to gain satisfaction.

It's more enjoyable and healthier to be driven by the carrot than the stick. To reduce stick-based motivation, we need to dismantle the mental frameworks that cause us suffering. These patterns push us to act just to relieve pain — for example, to stop feeling worthless, powerless, or angry. But even if we "succeed" in these pursuits, they won't truly eliminate the hurt. We still won't feel happy or satisfied. Only by disassembling these harmful frameworks can our happiness improve. Once we do, we're no longer driven by a need to ease pain but by a desire to enhance the happiness we already feel.

I acknowledge that, at an instinctive level, we respond more strongly to the stick than the carrot. We're often more motivated to act in order to avoid suffering, as past pain is easier to recall than past satisfaction. It's harder to feel driven to repeat activities we deeply enjoyed, since the memory of that satisfaction tends to be more muted. Unfortunately, we remember the stick far more vividly than the carrot.

Using the carrot alone to motivate us to start something new presents its own challenge. Without having experienced the pursuit, it's hard to imagine the satisfaction it might bring. We can't really imagine in detail the actual carrot we'll receive. It's like trying to guess how good something will taste without ever having tried it. All we have is the *possibility* of what that carrot could taste like. And because we can't imagine it in detail, the thought isn't inherently satisfying. As a result, it often fails to spark strong motivation. We can draw on similar past activities to get a rough sense, but that may not reflect the full potential of what lies ahead.

This can make us hesitant to shift away from stick-based motivation and rely purely on the carrot. But the stick creates a climate of fear that takes the enjoyment out of the activity, ultimately nullifying one of the main reasons we wanted to do it in the first place. For our satisfaction, it's better to train ourselves over time to be strongly motivated by the carrot in its various forms. Even if it's only the possibility of what it might taste like.

Train Ourselves to Put in Effort Even When Motivation Is Low

I think many of us have the mental habit of only putting in effort when we feel a strong sense of motivation. We believe we need to be filled with that intense drive to take action. Anything less, we don't try at all.

When I want to do something but feel little drive, I've found that if I try it anyway, I can often put in far more effort than I thought. I hadn't realized this before because, whenever I felt low motivation, I *assumed* I wouldn't be able to do much of anything.

When we let go of this assumption, we can build a new mental habit: choosing to apply ourselves even when our motivation is low. As we reinforce this behavior, we stop waiting for strong motivation before taking action. We stop underestimating how much effort we're capable of, even with low drive.

Other Influences on Our Motivation

While not exhaustive, two other factors come to mind that can affect our motivation.

The first is our energy level at a given point in the day. The more energy we have, the more motivated we tend to feel. Improving our diet and exercising regularly are the main ways we can influence this.

The second is our current interest in the activity. This can fluctuate for no clear reason and may not be something we can reliably manage.

THOUGHT PATTERNS THAT STIFLE THE CREATIVE SPIRIT

A few of the mental frameworks discussed in this book not only diminish our satisfaction but also discourage the creative spirit. Both in our desire to pursue artistic projects like music or painting, and in our willingness to experiment. Experimentation involves taking chances by combining elements that we haven't seen go together before. This kind of freedom can be found in both art and life.

The freedom to create, to experiment, and to play as we like is deeply satisfying. But when these thought patterns are present, we miss out on those emotional rewards. We'll now briefly revisit some of these harmful mental patterns to see how they hinder our creative spirit.

Our Ego Worries About Looking Foolish for Doing Something With Flaws

In Chapter 1, we discussed how the ego can prevent us from enjoying or valuing an activity if we perceive flaws in it. This was mainly in the context of consuming other people's creative work, such as TV or film. If we notice even minor flaws, we may be quick to dismiss the entire project.

When it comes to creating our own work, the ego's concern is even greater. If we fear looking silly for simply enjoying something flawed, that fear intensifies when we imagine others judging the shortcomings in what we create. Being highly critical is a double-edged sword. It's difficult to consistently judge others' work harshly without turning that same lens inward. As a result, we may hesitate to pursue creative projects at all. Deep down, we don't want to be on the receiving end of the kind of criticism we've often directed at others. We don't want to be labeled a fool in the same way that we have done.

But the greater fool is the one who lets the fear of looking silly prevent them from creating something at all. Especially given how deeply satisfying creative expression can be. In both the final result and the process, we learn so much about ourselves. When we avoid creativity out of fear that what we make will be flawed, we miss out on the emotional rewards and growth that come with it. No work is ever without flaws. While we may never fully realize our original vision, we can still bring it to life in an approximate way that is rewarding. Others may judge it, even mock it, but we shouldn't let their insecurities become our limitations. We shouldn't let other people's inhibitions hold us back.

To be clear, this isn't to say we should ignore flaws — in our work or anyone else's — or avoid thoughtful critique. Honest, constructive feedback helps us improve and grow. What matters is the spirit in which that criticism is given and received. It shouldn't be harsh, dismissive, or rooted in ego. We must remember that putting something creative into the world takes time, effort, sacrifice, and courage. A little humility and appreciation go a long way — both when evaluating the work of others and when creating our own.

Our Self-Worth Is Attached to Winning

In Chapter 10, we discussed how someone who believes they are inherently worthless may tie their self-esteem to winning competitions. When playing something like tennis, they may feel the need for victory in order to protect themselves from feelings of low self-worth. As a result, they often feel anxious or angry when they aren't winning.

Tying self-worth to winning limits the creative choices they're willing to make. For example, they may rely only on familiar, high-percentage shots that maximize their chances of success, avoiding more interesting or challenging plays. Their style becomes rigid, shaped by fear of failure rather than curiosity or enjoyment.

By contrast, someone whose self-esteem isn't tied to winning is free to experiment. This freedom allows them to explore different approaches based on what they find engaging or fun, rather than what gives them the best chance of victory. Their play style is shaped by interest and creativity, not by emotional pressure.

In addition, someone emotionally attached to winning is often focused solely on the end result. They fixate on the goal and struggle to engage with the moments leading up to it. Meanwhile, a person free from this emotional need can be more present during the activity, fully engaging with each moment rather than obsessing over the final outcome.

Ultimately, the person who isn't driven by an emotional need to win tends to enjoy the game more, regardless of whether they win or lose. The other, by contrast, may only understand how to play to win, not how to play for the enjoyment of playing.

SOME CLOSING REMARKS

If I were to summarize what this book is about, it would be this: inside each of us is a *doorway to happiness* and a much wider range of satisfying emotions. When we preserve and expand our mental freedom — whether as a child or as an adult — we experience greater and longer-lasting happiness.

The problem is, most of us haven't been given the right combination of words to keep that door open. More often, we've been handed the wrong ones. Ideas and beliefs that keep the door closed, or barely ajar, and only briefly. I like to think that by reading this book, you've now found the right words. Use them to keep the door open as wide as possible, for as long as possible. Do this so you can enjoy more of what each moment has to offer.

To arrive at these words, it was necessary to develop a unified theory of each person's reality — one grounded in the experience of the present moment. From that starting point, the other fundamentals flow: the desire for satisfaction, the nature of suffering, how we define the self and life, and how we understand right and wrong. While this model doesn't explain everything, it orders so many of the essentials in a way that I found to be elegant. Before then, a lot of my thoughts on these topics were in disarray and unpleasantly chaotic.

This understanding allows me to go into the world without entitlement and without expectation, both of which are vital to cultivating happiness in each moment.

To be clear, I don't mean I have low expectations; I mean I have none. After experiencing disappointment, many people adopt a "low expectations" mindset as a form of self-protection. But to me, that still assumes life is likely to disappoint. That outlook is subtly dissatisfying and can dull the richness of our experiences.

Instead, I believe it's better to enter each moment with no expectations at all, neither high nor low. That, to me, is a more freeing and satisfying way to live.

THANK YOU

Thanks for reading! If you enjoyed this book, I'd be grateful if you left a review. As an indie author, I depend on word of mouth and the support of readers like you to help others find my work.

If you'd like to share any thoughts with me directly, feel free to reach out at paul.daniel1590@gmail.com.

ALSO BY PAUL DANIEL

The Blindfolded Society: How We Progress When Mass
Self-Deception Holds Us Back

ABOUT THE AUTHOR

Paul Daniel has always been drawn to the question of happiness and how the mind can be both our greatest ally and our biggest obstacle. He's fascinated by how we can tinker with our thoughts to make life a little lighter and easier. Outside of writing, Paul enjoys spending time with his partner and two cats, reading sci-fi novels, and finding humor in life's contradictions.